change

organising
tomorrow,
today

Jay Naidoo

PENGUIN BOOKS

Published by Penguin Books
an imprint of Penguin Random House South Africa (Pty) Ltd
Reg. No. 1953/000441/07
The Estuaries No. 4, Oxbow Crescent, Century Avenue, Century City, 7441
PO Box 1144, Cape Town, 8000, South Africa
www.penguinrandomhouse.co.za

Penguin
Random House
South Africa

First published 2017

1 3 5 7 9 10 8 6 4 2

Publication © Penguin Random House 2017
Text © Jay Naidoo 2017

PUBLISHER: Marlene Fryer
MANAGING EDITOR: Robert Plummer
EDITOR: Genevieve Adams
PROOFREADER: Bronwen Maynier
COVER DESIGNER: Gretchen van der Byl
TEXT DESIGNER: Ryan Africa
TYPESETTER: Monique van den Berg
INDEXER: Sanet le Roux

Set in 11 pt on 15.5 pt Minion

Printed by **novus print**, a Novus Holdings company

MIX
Paper from
responsible sources
FSC
www.fsc.org   FSC® C022948

This book is printed on FSC® certified and controlled sources.
FSC (Forest Stewardship Council®) is an independent, international,
non-governmental organization. Its aim is to support environmentally sustainable,
socially and economically responsible global forest management.

ISBN 978 1 77609 180 5 (print)
ISBN 978 1 77609 181 2 (ePub)

*To future generations, who will surely make
wiser decisions for our only home, Mother Earth,
and for all species who share her social and spiritual fabric.*

Contents

Preface 1

1. The Summit 5
2. Race to the Bottom 19
3. The Spark 25
4. The Explosion 37
5. Organise or Starve 47
6. The Objective Objective 61
7. Building Solidarity 77
8. Managing Transition 95
9. The Challenge of Democracy 103
10. Lessons of the Lula Moment 111
11. The Power of the People 121
12. The World in Microcosm 133
13. Organising for a Planet 145
14. The Right to Feel Human 159
15. The Naledi Star 171
16. Real Change 187
17. Ancient Wisdom for Modern Times 201
18. Where to from Here? 209

Acknowledgements 219
Abbreviations 221
Notes 223
Index 227

We stand at a critical moment in Earth's history, a time when humanity must choose its future. As the world becomes increasingly interdependent and fragile, the future at once holds great peril and great promise. To move forward we must recognise that in the midst of a magnificent diversity of cultures and life forms we are one human family and one Earth community with a common destiny.

We must join together to bring forth a sustainable global society founded on respect for nature, universal human rights, economic justice, and a culture of peace. Towards this end, it is imperative that we, the peoples of Earth, declare our responsibility to one another, to the greater community of life, and to future generations.

– The Earth Charter, 29 June 2000

Preface

I HAVE LIVED A full life, immersed in the struggle for human dignity. Now, as I approach the last phase of my existence, I find myself looking forward to sharing it with my future grandchildren.

However, when I discussed this possibility with my twenty-one-year-old daughter Shanti, I was not expecting the answer she gave me. After looking at me for a few seconds, she said, with deep seriousness, 'Why would I consider bringing a child into a world you believe has destroyed our hope, which disembowels Mother Earth and where money and greed trounce human values you have spent your entire life fighting for?'

I was flabbergasted. I have been a social justice activist my entire life. As an opponent of apartheid, I fought in the trenches against prejudice and violence, and experienced victory in one of the greatest triumphs against injustice of the twentieth century. I have always seen it as my duty to make the world a better place for future generations, but now I was beginning to wonder whether I and other revolutionaries had failed in our efforts to provide South Africans with better opportunities, whether we had betrayed our children in the kind of world that we created for them.

Since that fateful conversation, I find myself waking up to the thought of these issues each day. It was literally my wake-up call.

Now I question every act that my generation has committed in the past. The proverb 'truth hurts but silence kills' now seems to hold a universal and absolute application in my reality.

The time has come for us to end this silence. Democracy is just a word. I am fully aware that people in South Africa and the rest of the world – especially our youth – have lost their trust in politicians. What is more, as my daughter so poignantly indicated, her generation has lost its hope in life, too. She is not alone in this belief.

It is evident that a new form of apartheid has taken root in world politics. The global experience now is of a broken political and economic system driven by insatiable self-indulgence that has created an unprecedented ecological crisis – one that threatens not only the human race, but all other life on the planet. An increasingly connected generation of young people around the world is questioning how much energy we as activists have spent on the internal bureaucratic practices of our comfortable careers, enjoying the privileged suburban lifestyles of a decreasing minority, while many members of the majority continue to suffer unemployment, poverty and the ongoing effects of global warming.

Their anger, legitimate and justified, will soon shatter the rock of privilege, indifference and ignorance that so many of us have sheltered under. I have travelled to other countries listening to people who live on the margins of opportunity, the planet's growing underclass, and seen in them the same anger that South Africans feel for their own government. They are correct in the belief that the system upheld by their leaders merely perpetuates injustice and corruption, even while it extends their lives. Many of them ask themselves, 'What is the point of living longer if I have no hope, no job and no future?'

There are many students and young activists, however, who are determined to avoid this reality at all costs. This connected group of individuals uses technology as a weapon which allows them to move quickly, often without the kind of bureaucratic and governmental structures that slow down older generations of activists. And while many older activists were consumed with the idea of governance in their struggle, simply changing the leadership of the old system, younger activists are looking to topple it, to transform it completely. Their experience of challenging the system is therefore usually met with scathing criticism, a demonisation of their views or, at worst, batons, tear gas and live ammunition.

This is not what the revolutionaries of the past fought for. To me, leadership, just like the democratic rights and institutions that South Africans have worked so hard to put in place, must be earned every day.

And so what I am sharing with you are my ideas for taking back the power that we have lost, lessons that I have gleaned from my personal voyage as an activist, labour leader, negotiator, reconciler, government minister and social entrepreneur who has worked on solving developmental issues in communities both locally and internationally. Some of these communities are attempting to dig their way out of poverty and degradation, and perhaps their experiences can serve as a guide for the kind of actions that can be taken by the next generation of activists fighting inequality.

This book is my attempt to answer the 'What is to be done?' question that faces many of them. It is a way of saying to my fellow activists, regardless of where you are in the world, that there is still a way to get to the top of the mountain. As a majority, we need not capitulate. We need never accept any status quo that entrenches privilege and deepens inequality, especially not in the twenty-first century.

Now is the time for every one of us to listen carefully, very carefully, to the voices crying out against the wrongs that are suffered every day. Building a brighter future must start with an honest intergenerational conversation. The political arrogance of my generation has taken us to the edge of a precipice of dashed expectations and an uncertain future which our youth will be forced to occupy.

We must come together if we want to redesign the world that our children will inherit.

The alternative is too terrible to contemplate.

1

The Summit

IN AUGUST 2014 I climbed a mountain.

As I stood on Africa's highest peak, looking down on the continent where I was born, that I love, I felt a sense of fathomless wonder at what I saw before me. I found myself pondering where it would be in a few decades – whether it would survive the next century, or for another millennium. Would it all still be here, I asked myself.

These were not merely academic or philosophical questions, but were firmly grounded in reality. The answers would affect me, my family and my friends, as well as my community, my country and, ultimately, the entire planet.

I soon realised that asking, 'Where will we be?' was just another way of saying, 'Where are we going?'

The ascent to the summit of Mount Kilimanjaro in Tanzania was a gruelling task.

No, that's an understatement. It was not only the most difficult physical challenge I have ever undertaken, it was the hardest physical challenge I could imagine anyone ever undertaking. The climb had been on my bucket list, and there were moments during the experience when I thought I would kick the bucket. Climbing a thousand metres a day while having to acclimatise to higher altitudes was a challenge I had thoroughly underestimated.

On the last night before the final ascent, at the base camp at Kibo, 4700 metres above sea level, my son Kami, who was accompanying me on the climb, spent time reassuring me. But I was nervous, especially after witnessing other climbers who had become seriously ill on the mountain being brought downhill on stretchers. Although I had trained for the ascent for months before, having wanted to complete the challenge before my sixtieth birthday on 20 December 2014, I had sprained my ankle only three weeks before I left for Tanzania and my foot was heavily wrapped up in a harness.

In that frozen world, I realised that nothing can really prepare you for such a task. This was not a Sunday outing with friends. It was ascending one of the highest natural structures in the world. I may have been in great shape for a sixty-year-old, but would that be enough to propel me to a height of nearly 6000 metres above sea level? This final reality check, the prospect of the ascent, terrified me. It terrified everyone at the camp waiting to set out on the trek.

Eating was difficult, remaining calm almost impossible. Our team organiser harangued us at mealtimes, 'Force it down! Those potatoes could mean the difference between reaching the summit or not.'

That night I struggled to sleep, tossing about in my sleeping bag until midnight, when my fellow mountaineers and I finally set out on our expedition. Beyond the hulking buttress of the mountain, the moon, like a ghost, haunted a sky sprinkled with stars.

Some groups had left before us. I could see the shadowy outline of their head torches illuminating the path at intervals. Uhuru Peak, a symbol of freedom,[1] loomed over us impressively. Between that point and heaven I imagined there to be nothing but aeroplanes, drones and satellites. Courage alone would not be enough to get us there; fitness, while important, was not a decisive element on the journey. Faith was certainly an advantage, and discipline and humil-

ity essential for tackling what lay ahead. More than anything, however, was the power that needed to be exercised by the mind over
the body – especially at my not-so-youthful age.

During the climb the Tanzanian guides were a great source of
comfort to my group. Experienced, patient, empathetic, optimistic,
I found them to be the salt of the earth. Spending each day with
them on the mountain brought back memories of my experiences
as a labour organiser in South Africa, when I stood side by side
with migrant workers outside the hostels or sugar mills. They were
community leaders shaped by demanding circumstances, hardship
and perseverance. And when I was in the union, I had felt safest
with people like them, breaking bread and braaiing meat over the
coals on cool early mornings. There was always an atmosphere of
honesty and social solidarity surrounding these occasions. We were
like a family, connected by the adversity we faced and in our joint
struggle for social justice.

On the mountain I felt that same sense of security with my
guides Julio, Salvatore, John, Alex and Alifayo. '*Pole, pole,*' they
quietly reminded me throughout the ascent. Pronounced 'poli, poli',
it is Kiswahili for 'slowly, slowly'. One step at a time, one breath at
a time. *Smiley, smiley* – revere the experience. *Sippy, sippy* – take a
regular drink of water along the way. All through the ascent, these
words became our mantra. They brought lightness and cheer to
each task that we completed.

After a while I turned to music, taking out my earphones and
distracting myself with my favourite rhythms from Johnny Clegg
and Angélique Kidjo. But after hours of seemingly endless upward
shuffling, pausing only long enough to moisten my mouth with tea,
I felt my body starting to revolt against the intense physical effort.
Simply breathing was becoming a strenuous exercise, although resting for a few moments was not an option either; nor was allowing
myself to dwell on my discomfort.

Instead, I drew strength from the examples of two iconic African leaders: Tanzania's Julius Kambarage Nyerere, known as Mwalimu ('teacher' in Kiswahili), and Nelson Rolihlahla Mandela, lovingly known as Tata Madiba in South Africa and my father in all but blood.

Both men had displayed immense courage and resilience in their personal struggles for the independence of their countries, and the manner in which they lived their lives has shaped much of my thinking. In December 2013 Mandela was buried in the Eastern Cape among the hills where he was born and where he had wandered as a young shepherd. His death, though long expected, had left me shattered. Like Nyerere, Mandela was successful in guiding his nation to sovereign independence from white rule, and was a symbol of sacrifice and unrelenting commitment to the service of his people.

As the founding fathers of their respective nations, Nyerere and Mandela have earned the respect and admiration of millions because their motives, while not always popular, were always pure. Leadership to them was both a skill and an art, carried out in a tireless pursuit of service, of building communities, and of promoting unity among their people. *Public service for these exemplary leaders was never a business opportunity.*

Reaching Uhuru was therefore a personal act of gratitude to these men for the selflessness they demonstrated in their individual struggles for freedom. It would be foolhardy to diminish the pioneering roles they played in the particular period of history they were born into, even while it is correct to question some of the decisions they made. They never claimed to be saints, and I do not canonise them. But as humble leaders of Africa's battle against colonisation and apartheid, they have heavily influenced my politics and those of many other politicians and leaders.

Mandela's and Nyerere's unwavering commitment to their people's interests cannot be questioned either, even though it is inarguable that they made mistakes, and sometimes very serious ones. The same qualification applies to every other leader I discuss in this book. Politicians, after all, are human beings and frequently trip up, just as all people do – just as I have done. I have tried to learn from my errors, and am often reminded that the fight for power is always easier than the exercise of power. It is those who fail to understand the context in which leaders live who are bound to repeat the blunders of the past. My Kilimanjaro expedition consequently left me wondering what Mandela and Nyerere would have made of the state of Africa today and the circumstances which are shaping our present; what they would have thought of the Africa Rising narrative, which perpetuates a belief in rapid and continued economic growth on the continent while only focusing on the needs of an elitist class, and the doomsday beliefs of Afro-pessimists, who believe that all is lost for our continent as long as the black majority rules it.

Opposing viewpoints can promote robust, open discussions that inspire new ideas and beliefs. It seems necessary in these complex times to consider more than one or two categorical viewpoints about a continent with fifty-four countries, each with a story of their own.

At the same time little has been done to unite competing narratives within these countries, to fulfil the requirements of the continued revolution that will bring about 'nationhood' in South Africa, Tanzania or anywhere else in a world torn apart by diversity and the interests of those who benefit from this division between countries and people. Have we done enough to build on the foundations that Mandela and Nyerere constructed in their struggle for justice; to forge the necessary coherence, instil the right values and repair the deep injustices of the past? It is with piercing clarity that I have come to realise just how little has truly changed for the majority of the world's people.

I continued my ascent, my thoughts taking on a rhythm of their own, the refrain of my shuffle becoming 'One step for Tata Madiba, one step for Mwalimu'. It was the only thing that gave me the courage to endure the journey.

One step for Tata Madiba. One step for Mwalimu.

As the night wore on and the climb became harder, my mind began forming strange thoughts. I wondered about the journey of life and whether any of us are ever really alone. By virtue of living in nation states we are surrounded by people who ostensibly share our values and our outlooks.

And as humans move from villages and towns to big cities, geographical boundaries start to blur as well. We live on top of one another, sharing backyards in the crowded chaos of slums and townships while just a short distance away, behind high walls and electric fences, sit large bubbles of opulence occupied by the wealthy, or the skyscrapers in which corporations elevate themselves. The spaces between the ridiculously rich and painfully poor are sometimes only a matter of a few kilometres.

An array of high-tech devices further connects these disparate groups. They inform us at every opportunity of the whereabouts of our friends, what they are eating and where they are doing so. If there were a Starbucks at the top of Kilimanjaro, my smartphone would have recommended it to me at the moment of my arrival.

Governments and corporations, both foreign and our own, use these technologies to trace our movements, record our phone calls and calculate algorithms that predict our shopping and citizen behaviour. A digital fabric envelops the world, not to empower citizens and connect us to a higher purpose, but to allow our governments to create a surveillance world that disempowers us. It sells us material goods we do not need and cannot afford. We swoon over social media sites which further advance a zombie uniformity, diminishing who we are, undermining our self-esteem and reducing us to poor photocopies of Western cultural norms. And all of this despite what I know about Africa as having no one story, of being a patchwork quilt of colour, cuisine, culture, joy and sorrow, of generosity and brutality. It is unlike any other place in the world – a veritable cauldron of contradictions and turbulence.

Yet we discard our ancient knowledge, culture, language and

history – things we should be proud of – and as Africans are made to feel inferior. We want to be American, European, anything other than who we are, and this despite living on a continent that is the cradle of all humanity. But it is precisely our individual connections to ancient knowledge, eternal truths and past generations that steady us as we build our future. Africans should be harnessing the digital revolution to create our own content and global symbols, to celebrate our own history and mythology so that we can continue to build our futures.

Humans today make up the most connected generation in the history of our species, and, as a result, we are never alone, not for a second. But so many of us, regardless of where we are from, still feel disconnected from others, and often lonely and friendless. Around the world, groups of people speak of being under-represented, believing their governments and leaders to be indifferent to their problems. It is ironic that having half a dozen social media sites at our fingertips does not prevent us from feeling entirely voiceless.

Why do we feel like we're climbing the mountain all on our own?

As a union organiser, I was a witness to the inherent connection that exists between Africans regardless of colour and culture, as well as our capacity to unite around common struggles to fight the system that sought to steal our humanity. It seems as if we have forgotten that we are capable of this. In the long history of resistance against the shared enemies of imperialism, racism and capitalism, our current generation of activists seems to be the flaw in the pattern, holding no unified or distinct position on how to oppose the new manifestations of these forces. It is clearly time for a shift in consciousness. As Africans, we need to come together and restore the ties that once made us the West's most feared enemy. We have to bring back to the fore our ancient knowledge and beliefs – our traditions of solidarity, compassion and respect for the earth as encompassed in the philosophy of *ubuntu* – 'I am because we are'. A connection between the head, the heart and the spirit.

As I scaled the last agonising thousand metres of Kilimanjaro's northern face, I thought back to my own experiences as a boy in apartheid South Africa and the hardships I faced under racist rule. The enemy was all around me in the form of a political system that refuted the idea that black people such as myself had rights. It was a regime that deprived us of our human dignity and made us mere commodities in a cheap labour market controlled by a privileged white minority.

We fought to make ourselves heard, to propose to the regime a set of universal truths that acknowledged the advent of peace only when every South African citizen had the right to vote for the leader of their choice in a democratic, non-racial, non-sexist state. When the government refused to listen, we fought. And when they fought back, we fought harder. As activists, we refused to collaborate in our own oppression. Step by step, *pole, pole,* we inched our way towards freedom.

So in 1990, when Nelson Mandela was released from prison after serving twenty-seven years for opposing the state, the struggle, it seemed, was all but over.

At least, that's what we thought.

Mandela's release signalled the beginning of an irreversible advance for black South Africans. It was the first step towards us reclaiming our dignity. We were suddenly on the road to ending the inhumanity of racial segregation and reconstructing a society that would work for all. We thought we had won the fight. And in many ways we did.

But it turns out that even when you have reached the summit of the mountain, you are not done climbing.

So much has happened since apartheid ended in 1994 – a lot of it good, some of it bad, and some of it really terrible. The promise of a 'freer world' that emerged in the early nineties after the collapse of the Berlin Wall is losing its luminous potential and rapidly disappearing. People in South Africa, and many others around the world, are now witnessing the resurrection of an old and terrible phenomenon: apartheid by a different name.

We live in an age of rampant inequality. While trying to breathe in the oxygen-deprived mountain air, I could still recall the numbers by heart, including those from a 2010 study that revealed how 388 billionaires owned as much wealth as half of the world's population. By 2016 that number had narrowed, with sixty-two individuals sharing the same wealth as more than 3.5 billion people.[2]

As more money becomes concentrated in the hands of a few, we will continue to see a widening of the gap between the rich and the poor. Economic catch-up in countries such as China and India tends to exacerbate this trend in the developing world. It is clear that a rich person from one of these nations often has more in common with a wealthy individual in the United States or Europe than with their fellow citizens. The reality is that the geographic certainty of the nation state is fast evaporating.

In an effort to halt the spread and devastation of poverty, the United Nations (UN) Millennium Development Goals were adopted in 2000 with the goal of halving the number of people living in absolute poverty by 2015. It has become the most successful anti-poverty movement in history, accomplishing its goal of decreasing the number of people living on $1.25 a day by half, to 836 million in 2015.[3]

But how do we disaggregate these numbers before the grey suits claim victory and raise their champagne glasses?

Statistically, economic growth in China seems to be the primary driver of this decrease in world poverty. In the last three decades, more than half a billion Chinese have been lifted out of impoverishment, meaning that more than half of the people benefiting from the UN's 'successful' reduction of world poverty come from one country. Yet it was not ideology but pragmatism determined by local realities that shaped the model of Chinese growth – the result of a state-driven programme rather than the work of a fabled free market.

Chinese leaders made sure to reject the 'shock therapy' tactics employed by the World Bank and the International Monetary Fund (IMF) to transform the Soviet Union when the Berlin Wall collapsed, which only exacerbated the economic crises in these countries. But China's leadership has also become aware of the tremendous ecological cost of their economic growth model, and this is what makes China the most fascinating place to watch as it tackles the necessary adoption of renewable energy. I for one am convinced that government policy and decision-makers around the world, with China leading the move, will eventually prioritise the environment above gross domestic product (GDP) growth on a scale never seen before. It will be in response to the catastrophic impact of pollution and global warming on the health of billions of people and on the world's natural environment.

Irregular rainfall and persistent droughts are already major drivers of a rising food and water crisis that continues to debilitate the social development of many impoverished communities, leaving many people displaced and without homes, or dead. In October 2015 the World Bank raised the international poverty line to $1.90, but I question the authority of this institution in determining how little it takes for other people to survive every day. It is highly unlikely that the bureaucrats who have created these financial models, sitting in their air-conditioned offices, would ever be able to raise their own families on such a pittance, so why is it acceptable that millions of other people have to do so? This scientific approach to the suffering of others is similar to the thoughtless indifference shown in the 'Let them eat cake' school of thought of imperial France – the kind of attitude that many world leaders seem to have adopted towards the impoverished inhabitants of their countries.

They drive by in 'blue light brigades' while their subjects scrabble through the garbage for food. We vote, but our votes don't count. When governments win elections, they rarely carry out the responsibilities that form part of their mandate. It becomes evident soon afterwards that voting campaigns were merely closed popularity contests funded by individuals and businesses with selfish interests and suitcases full of cash. Once the vote is won, very little or no concern is displayed for forming policy or delivering services that will provide the 'better life' that was promised to the people.

These corrupt elites masquerade as leaders while creating patronage systems that undermine our public institutions. They control the allocation of public resources and opportunities, distributing them to individuals for their narrow political and material gain. The result is a cancer of crony capitalism that gnaws away at the heart of the nation, sabotaging any attempt by government to fulfil its obligations or uphold the tremendous victories of our freedom struggle. I have witnessed this with my own eyes and heard the cries of our people who despair at the arrogance and egotism of their leaders.

None of this has occurred in isolation, however, and as citizens of a democratic South Africa we must admit our share of the blame. Somewhere along the line we decided to outsource our engagement as citizens to our leaders, placing the power that had freed our country solely into their hands. We believed that the democratic institutions that brought a new order to the nation would hold strong, but it turns out that every government has the capacity to be seduced by the prospect of absolute power, as well as the abuse thereof, and our government was certainly no different.

Freedom, as it turns out, requires eternal vigilance, and the gift of freedom does not entail doing what we want whenever we want.

Forgetting this was a terrible mistake. Democracy is a priceless gift. And although much has improved since the days of apartheid, another kind of reality has begun to intrude on the beauty and promise of our country. The renewed implementation of exclusionary practices from our past has created a rampantly unequal society that now threatens to explode into violence with every street protest and political scandal that makes headline news.

The barriers that exist between the rich and the poor have become dangerous and unsustainable. They threaten not only the societies we claim to value, but the very planet on which we live. To break them down, we need to create a new world order that no longer privileges one group of people over another because of their wealth, status, nationality, gender, religion or culture. We need to bring together the many who suffer injustice as a result of the rules and ideology enforced by a privileged few, and create a set of unified values that calls for peace, justice and human dignity.

My walk up Kilimanjaro reminded me of how integral organisation and preparedness are in undertaking any task, especially a global movement. Throughout the journey I was struck by the meticulousness of our guides in their preparation for the excursion. They knew what our kits needed, when we had to rest, the correct pathways to take up the mountain, and how to assist us with our breathing and actually surviving the climb. They encouraged, coaxed and pushed us forward, always emphasising that we were useless as individuals but had a much better chance of success if we stuck together. They fully embraced the overall purpose of their job, which was to get us to the top of the mountain and, most importantly, to get us back down alive. Alongside Kami, my son, who fuelled my courage, they were mentors, therapists and social workers, and were very often the crutch I needed to get through the arduousness of the entire undertaking.

I was like that once. My existence was all about organisation. As a member of the modern trade union movement under the umbrella of the Congress of South African Trade Unions (COSATU), I contributed to the militant struggle for progressive workers' rights, protesting alongside workers against the political system that was subjugating us. It was not so long ago that I, along with masses of my comrades, went to war against this foe that often seemed unconquerable. And yet we succeeded in defeating it, always keeping in mind that the battles against inequality, poverty and underdevelopment were far from over and would continue to present massive challenges to activists and social movements.

My fighting skills were honed by the same people I represented, who showed me how to go to war and to know what I was warring against. The most important lesson I learnt from them, however, was how to listen and to connect with other people. It was thus as a collective that we were able to defeat the legal system that had sustained the apartheid regime.

It might be painful for me to admit, but it is undeniably evident that South Africans' walk to freedom is far from over. There are many more mountains to climb. And yet, even while faced with all of this gloom, there are hundreds of positive stories from local communities I have encountered that tell of their determination to organise around a common goal and to improve their way of living. You will find millions more. We need to connect these dots of hope, to build bridges which embrace solidarity and compassion, and cultivate a new generation of leadership that connects the head, hands, heart and soul.

Not all the answers can be found within these pages. This is a mission in which we should all participate. I have stood on the roof of Africa. I have seen with my own eyes the immeasurable beauty of this continent and understood what *Uhuru* truly means. There is no reason why anyone in Africa or the rest of our global village should accept anything less than equality and human well-being under the rule of law.

One step at a time. *Pole, pole.* It is time to start climbing again.

2

Race to the Bottom

S OME MOUNTAINS ARE literal, and some are figurative.
During apartheid I was constantly climbing my own metaphorical Kilimanjaro, and there were occasions when the peak of the mountain, where justice reigned, seemed permanently out of reach. I felt this frustration particularly during the early seventies when everyone around me, including my parents, bore an air of resignation towards the system, as if there was no means of defeating it. Their sense of hopelessness was compounded by the fact that many fighters in the struggle had been either forced into exile or imprisoned, including Nelson Mandela, who had been condemned to life imprisonment in 1964 for high treason.

Growing up, I was not always aware that the life I was destined to lead had already been determined for me by the colour of my skin. It did not matter if we were classified Indians, coloureds or Africans; we all suffered oppression to varying degrees under apartheid. Yet there was a part of me that knew something was wrong. I was a person, but in apartheid South Africa I was a non-person – simply because I was not white. This aspect of my existence encroached on all of my experiences, revealing its most insidious side in 1958 when my family was evicted from our home in Greenwood Park, Durban, under the Group Areas Act. Passed in 1950, four years before I was born, this Act gave the apartheid government the authority to enforce a brutal separation of the races in communities throughout South Africa. People of 'colour' were removed from areas which were considered 'black spots' in the exclusive territory of white South Africa. The outcome was the mass destruction of stable and unified communities in one of the largest forced removals in modern history, which saw the expulsion of 3.5 million black South Africans from their homes between 1960 and 1983.[1]

Racism, however, was merely the mask concealing the white government's real motivation for segregationist rule. Racial discrimination was, and still is, a very handy tool for carrying out capitalist aims and policies in South Africa, and forms the basis of cheap labour systems buttressed by extreme exploitation of the working class.

In apartheid South Africa legalised racial segregation absolved white capital from any obligation to care for migrant workers' families. It forced the black majority to carry the hated *dompas*, or passbook, everywhere they went, and to submit to a curfew that prevented them from moving through towns and cities at night. Black people were prohibited from buying land and living alongside whites, forced, instead, to occupy the fringes of society where jobs were scarce and the schools were bad. Racial discrimination infringed on even the most mundane aspects of our lives, determining where we could sit on buses or trains, and which movie theatres, dancehalls or hospitals we could visit. The existence of African people was determined only by their capacity to serve the white minority.

Our birth rights were stolen by a government that obtained its power from the highly racist colonial regimes of the Dutch and then the English in the seventeenth and eighteenth centuries. Cecil John Rhodes, the English mining magnate and prime minister of the Cape Colony from 1890 to 1896, famously captured the ethos of his country's reasons for coming to the 'New World' when he said, 'We must find new lands from which we can easily obtain raw materials and at the same time exploit the cheap slave labour that is available from the natives of the colonies ... The colonies would also provide a dumping ground for the surplus goods produced in our factories.'

The entire history of colonial conquest in South Africa was driven by a war against the indigenous population, the destruction of local culture and knowledge systems, and a strategy of land dispossession, all of which were conceived even before the first white settlers set foot on the African continent. Under the tutelage of the British Crown, the white state was able to legalise its rape and plunder of the country through the 1913 Land Act, seizing 87 per cent of the land and forcing black people into Bantustans – undersized reservoirs of undeveloped earth that fed cheap labour to the mines and farms. Black men were the ill-fated targets of this exploitative system, deprived of land on which to raise their cattle and forced to pay a range of taxes for their huts, cattle and for polls. They had no other choice but to leave their homes for the cities and take jobs that paid negligible wages which kept them destitute.

When the Afrikaner-controlled National Party beat the liberal United Party in the whites-only election of 1948, the practice of racial segregation was thereafter institutionalised as apartheid. Much like the so-called Jim Crow segregationist laws in the American South, racism became the law of the land and the basis for the government's segregation of black and white citizens.

Yet in spite of the reasoning behind apartheid's promotion of a physical separation of the races, race by itself is mostly an abstract concept, based primarily on the insubstantial idea of physical appearance. As one of the only existing subspecies of hominid alive today, all 7.3 billion *Homo sapiens* on the planet are more similar biologically than we are different. In fact, from a genetic point of view, we are 99.9 per cent identical. The concept of race had to be socially constructed because, scientifically, it does not exist and cannot be read in the human genome. It is an idea that has been cultivated in our heads for centuries, shaped by society's prejudices and projections, and not borne in our genes. In scientific terms, the only race that really exists is the human race.

The polygenist Christoph Meiners is considered the father of scientific racism and was one of the first people to suggest that each 'race' had separate origins. In his book *The Outline of History of Mankind*, published in 1785, this warped theorist argues that humanity can be divided into a 'beautiful white race' and an 'ugly Black race'. So it was during the period of so-called European Enlightenment that a cabal of white men posing as 'natural philosophers' introduced the pernicious notion of race as fact and gave justification to colonists for destroying indigenous cultures in other countries. Their theories provided Europeans with the rationale that they were superior to peoples with darker skin and had to civilise them – a task they believed was their God-given right and responsibility.

By investing their ideas with moral and religious authority, they could then rightfully insinuate that persons who were not white were lesser than them, mere commodities to be traded and abused for the benefit of their white overlords.

It is probably not surprising that such perceptions on the physical and intellectual inferiority of persons who are not white – ideas that were not only propagated by the apartheid government but upheld as law – had a profound effect on the way I saw myself. I was humiliated and broken, and actually felt inferior. Growing up in racist South Africa, being subject to its laws and daily abuses, I became increasingly enraged. I wanted either to fight the perpetrators of this injustice or give up and turn to social delinquency like so many hopeless souls do to escape their pain. But there was also a bigger part of me that wanted neither of these things; I dreamt, instead, of changing the matrix and altering the entire system.

Such ambitions always seemed futile, never based in any reality of which I was aware. Realistically, how was one skinny 'Indian' boy from the outskirts of the teeming port city of Durban supposed to go to war with the regime? I would be dashed to pieces in a second, torn limb from limb. It seemed I had no viable options.

I was stuck.

There isn't usually some deep theoretical concept that prompts people to change. There is no road map or plan. As history has taught us, it is more often a flash of lightning that inspires transformation or reform.

Before the revolutions that swept through much of the Arab world in 2010, no one would have believed that Mohamed Bouazizi, a twenty-six-year-old fruit seller in Tunisia, would set the Arab region alight after literally doing so to himself. His sacrifice, motivated by his anger at a status quo that denied him the dignity of work, instigated numerous other conflagrations across North Africa and the Middle East, resulting in the downfall of ruthless dictators who had once seemed all but invincible.

A conversation I had with Aya Chebbi, a young activist and blogger who participated in the uprisings in Tunisia, reminded me that such events should not only be considered from a broad perspective, as the actions of a single or pre-defined group of people. Chastising me for using the term 'Arab Spring' to describe the uprising, she pointed out, 'It's the typical Western hijacking of our struggle again. Ours is the revolution for human dignity. We are Africans before we are Arabs.'

I understood where she was coming from. Time and again, the corporate media and political commentators have tried to place the struggles of Africans into neat boxes that allow for easier Western analysis of these issues. Revolutions and uprisings, sometimes even a multitude occurring at the same time, are seen as the result of a single world-changing event, or as being incited by a powerful charismatic leader. While this can be the case, there are modern movements which were motivated by a build-up of events, years of discontent and anger, and remain leaderless because the desire for change exists on a large scale. The Arab protests and Occupy Wall Street campaign are two examples of such leaderless movements, intended to inspire masses of people to come together to fight a shared injustice rather than rally around a single catalyst or an individual.

Of course, this does not necessarily protect them from being hijacked and becoming fragmented by the agendas of a few players looking to fill up a new vacuum for control. In this context, the movement, once anchored to a simple but ground-breaking idea, a signature image or conclusive act, is divided, and the chances of its success greatly diminished. As organisers and activists, our main duty is to learn how to organise for the short, medium and long term to prevent this from happening.

The lynchpin idea is the spark, the impulse or provocation that is required for change. When I was a rebellious, angry youth in apartheid South Africa, I was in need of an idea that would spark me into action, inspire me to utilise my rage as a tool of activism. I soon learnt that the spark just needs the tinder of dissent in a repressive, unequal society to eventually catch alight.

This lesson was taught to me by none other than one of South Africa's master fire-lighters.

3

The Spark

IT IS A hot summer's afternoon in one of Durban's Indian districts in Reservoir Hills. The area's local Lutheran Church is the setting of a meeting by the South African Students' Organisation (SASO), which I will be attending.

The year is 1968, a heady time for global student politics. Massive protests have ripped through major cities in Europe and across the United States over unjust workers' laws, the violation of black Americans' civil rights and the war in Vietnam. Socialism is gaining more ground among political activists as the egalitarian alternative to the period's divisive politics, which pit powerful governments against their citizens and motivate political oppression and violence. It is a period that has seen a rise in the number of radical or militant movements in countries around the world, including the 1964 coup d'état in Brazil, black consciousness in South Africa in the mid-1960s, and the Black Panthers in the United States in 1966.

As a black teenager in apartheid South Africa I am, of course, unaware of these momentous events. There is no internet, no television and everything, especially information, is controlled by the state.

But I had grown up with an awareness that something was wrong, the shame I felt about my skin colour and my fear of white people eventually inspiring my rage against the system. I want to be part of the unrest, to join those South Africans who feel my pain and want it gone. So with my brother Logie, who is a member of SASO, I visit the church hall to hear a speech by a rising star in the anti-apartheid movement. The venue is crammed with people and cars pull up outside, expelling large men, white and Indian, who are holding weapons. Known as the Special Branch, these men hold a menacing vigil outside the hall, trying to intimidate anyone who dares venture inside.

Inside the hall a man walks onto the stage. He is young, charismatic, and looms over all of us imposingly. Within him seems to burn a fire so powerful that we can almost feel it consuming us.

'*Amandla!*' he shouts. Power!

Everyone in the hall responds in unison, '*Ngawethu!*' To the people!

The room is stuffy and crowded, but its atmosphere is electric. I am mesmerised by the man's fearlessness.

'Black man,' he says, addressing every one of us. 'You are on your own. We have nothing to lose except our chains. There is only black and white in this country. There is no middle ground. We must take a stand. We are either for justice and freedom, or apartheid and servitude.'

The man saying this was Stephen Bantu Biko, the anti-apartheid activist and founder of the Black Consciousness Movement (BCM) in South Africa. After hearing him speak, I found myself looking at the struggle from a new perspective.

Biko's thesis was one of 'us' versus 'them'. There were two sides to the conflict – those imposing injustice, and those fighting for justice. Along with everyone who was not white, I was oppressed under apartheid laws. It did not matter that I was Indian, or that my ancestors were from India. I was a black South African and had to join other black South Africans if I hoped to overcome the forces that were oppressing us.

After this realisation, I found myself exhausted by the petty racism of the Indian community and decided to break free from such old harmful stereotypes. Any notions I might have previously had of effecting change only for people of my own ethnicity were gone. The idea of barriers existing between those seeking to bring down apartheid had been advanced by the government to keep us divided. As Biko emphasised, we were stronger as a unified force. I could no longer live with an articulation of multiracialism or the so-called thesis of Africans, coloureds, Indians and whites.

Biko inspired me to commit to working with other South Africans in the anti-apartheid struggle, and I began participating in acts of individual rebellion – one of the millions of oppressed trying to make my views known. Biko helped us find our voices, gave agency to our anger, and espoused none of the narrow chauvinistic tenets of nationalism and tribalism that are still emerging in current political debates in the country.

That meeting in the church hall was the first and only occasion I heard Steve Biko speak in person. It was the only time I needed to. His genius lay in giving black South Africans a political vision, one that allowed us to see ourselves without shackles. By sharing his impossible dream of freedom in our lifetime, Biko lit up our minds and rewired our synapses. The world was suddenly a different place as we confronted that interminable question: What to do about it all?

Biko stated that the choice was simple. There was no elaborate business plan to present to governments and philanthropic foundations, no PowerPoint presentation or 'log frames' of rich donors seeking to buy themselves a legacy.

His words still echo in my mind as if I had heard them yesterday: Be inspired! Be fearless! Once the dream has been dreamt, it cannot be undreamed.

In almost every respect Biko was a human spark, the kind of man who can ignite an entire movement, handing over a solitary torch that is carried forward by millions. You cannot plan for these moments, nor can they be manufactured. Once they arrive on the scene, there is no erasing them, no matter how hard you try.

Biko reminded us that the struggle for fundamental transformation is long-term. It is not some reality TV show or Hollywood movie – entertaining to watch but ultimately an unrealistic reel of celluloid.

The directive he gave was so revolutionary, so potentially destructive to the ruling regime, that it did everything in its power to try to extinguish that flame. In September 1977 Biko, who had been arrested in the previous month, was executed in police custody after being beaten and denied proper medical care by security police.

His murder was the white establishment's attempt to silence him, but it only served to make his ideas all the more powerful. Those of us who identified with his message were unwavering in our efforts to share it with all others determined to fight the apartheid system. His message transcended silence. It transcended death.

And yet Biko, while espousing such powerful ideas, was also mindful of their limitations. In a television interview he agreed to in the early 1970s, he was asked whether the 'vast number of blacks' who had suffered under apartheid would be willing to concede to a non-racial society without visiting revenge on their former oppressors. Biko, who understood what was required both from those who engaged in a struggle and from those against whom it was aimed, would not be drawn into the trap.

> We believe that it is the duty of the vanguard political movement which brings about change to educate people's outlooks. In the same way that blacks have never lived in a socialist economic system, they've got to learn to live in one. In the same way that they've always lived in a racially divided society, they've got to learn to live in a non-racial society. They've got many things to learn. And all this must be brought to them, and explained to the people by the vanguard movement which is leading the revolution.[1]

But it is almost as if Biko is asking, 'What vanguard movement?' How do you initiate a vanguard movement while under the watchful eye of an authoritarian and repressive regime? There are certainly many prerequisites, including deciding what it will look like, who its members and leaders will be, and the negotiation and settlement of its policies.

This notion of an applicability of ideals was missing from the BCM philosophy and Biko's advancement of it. His brilliance had lain in the simple beauty of his thoughts and words. It was a revolution of ideas, taught through pure energy and with an unwavering commitment to the cause. Even in modern times, it continues to inspire a whole new generation of revolutionaries.

In the end, however, black consciousness was a philosophy that only offered a solution for living your life with dignity. It gave its followers confidence, but it was not a vanguard movement that provided a real strategy for forming a transformative collective undertaking.

Those of us who were prepared to protest had been given the ideas and beliefs that formed the ideology of our cause. But without the knowledge of what to do with them, we were still offering little to the struggle. When Biko was assassinated, our situation became even more uncertain. He had offered us hope, but now we were on our own. How would we continue to fight?

Looking back, I now understand that our oppression was about simple concepts. Apartheid was plain wrong, and everyone who lived under its rule knew it. You did not have to be black, liberal, a communist or a member of the African National Congress (ANC) to realise that depriving the majority of a country's citizens of basic rights was unjust. Even the bad guys knew it was an evil system. This was why the apartheid government built a massive army to protect itself from its black subjects and militarised every aspect of daily life. Anyone with a touch of sanity knew that the system could not, and would not, last. Their hatred for us could only take them so far.

For those of us participating in the struggle, it was easy to see the problem of apartheid from this perspective. It was about black and white.

The tough part was understanding how to organise ourselves so we could reclaim our rights. That was where Biko came in. Using plain language in the vernacular of the streets, he asked us to remove the shackles that had been placed on our thinking, to realise that 'our minds as the oppressed are the main weapon in the hands of the oppressor'.

He reminded us of our essential humanity.

We are all born free, he said, and should be able to live that way.

But knowing this did not mean that it was necessarily going to happen. Biko, in his righteousness, ultimately did not free us, although he helped us understand that freedom was something we had to achieve by ourselves.

Like the previous generation of resistance fighters, including Nelson Mandela, Govan Mbeki, and Walter and Albertina Sisulu, Biko never presented himself as a messiah. If he had lived, his primary mission would probably have been to transform the Black Consciousness Movement into a more organised force. Perhaps it would have been militant in nature, or perhaps not. The point is that something had to happen next. Something always has to happen if you want change.

Biko had offered a concrete analysis of the problems inherent to apartheid rule. The black consciousness philosophy helped him show fellow activists how to rally around a cause that would unify our objectives and impair the apartheid government's attempts to subdue us. Previous resistance fighters here and abroad also utilised ideology and the belief in a shared goal to organise their activities.

The modern political struggle in South Africa was underscored by the ideological goal of creating equality and justice in society.

It crystallised the simple message of freedom around which we organised and built our new vision. This aspect of the struggle is certainly not a new one and dates back to the colonial era, although early histories of the range of liberation movements in South Africa are hard to come by. The oldest might not be easily discernible given that the history books were written by the same people who were doing the oppressing. But it is essential to acknowledge that black people never sat back and dolefully accepted their enslavement, regardless of who they were fighting. Whether it was the colonial iteration of segregation or, later, 'grand apartheid', the fight for freedom started almost the moment the first white settlers landed at the Cape in 1652. South African history is littered with accounts of valiant battles against invading white settlers. But spears and courage were no match for gunpowder and cannonballs, nor for missionaries armed with religious scriptures to convert indigenous 'savages'.

Black South Africans also attempted peaceful forms of protest against the white government, using non-violence as the basis of their activism during much of the first half of the anti-apartheid struggle. The ANC, formed in 1912, took inspiration from Gandhi's strategy of passive resistance to obtain rights for Indians in both South Africa and India. Following the inception of apartheid in 1948, the party set out its campaign of defiance and direct action through nonaggressive but more militant forms of confrontation than Gandhi's, using mass action, strikes, demonstrations, boycotts and acts of defiance to oppose the government.

One stream of thought that reinforced this campaign was the idea of non-racialism, popularised in the 1980s by the United Democratic Front (UDF), the Mass Democratic Movement (MDM) and the Congress of South African Trade Unions. As general secretary of COSATU from 1985 to 1993, I endorsed a non-racial approach to the struggle because it upheld the notions of 'dual' and 'people's power'. This made sense because our goal at COSATU was to be out in the trenches organising our people, not in the meeting room engaging in semantics.

Our strategic outlook was that people who are organised are the motivating force behind change. Organisation requires forging alliances around a set of core demands; empowering communities to build their struggles around these demands; and strengthening negotiations with existing institutions such as government departments, universities, workplaces and even banks. All of this occurs while communities develop their own self-organised counter-institutions such as civic movements, education and health committees, and unions.

The impact that this kind of community and institutional organisation can have on unifying a broad spectrum of interests was most forcefully displayed in the #RhodesMustFall campaign of 2015. Beginning in March of that year, thousands of students at the University of Cape Town (UCT) set out to have the statues of racist colonialist Cecil John Rhodes removed from campuses and public spaces in South Africa. The protest, which lasted months, drew attention to the anger that so many black students feel about the prejudice that still shapes academia in formerly white universities as well as the economy.

The campaign struck an emotional chord with me. If I were a black student from Khayelitsha or some other township at UCT, I would be at the forefront of this movement, determined to help overthrow a symbol of the racist and exclusionary history of our country. I would want to be part of the struggle that reminds our white and black elites of the rampant poverty, unemployment and hopelessness that exists on the outskirts of their leafy suburbs; that the legacy of apartheid remains deeply embedded in our social fabric, with our public institutions and state controlled by the vested interests of a corporate elite. The student resistance is a call out against this exclusion and the lack of transformation that has continued since the start of democracy in 1994.

It is also the beginning of a larger struggle. Student leaders, understanding that change occurs only when the oppressed can see themselves outside of the viewpoint of the oppressor, declared that 'The removal of the statue will not be the end of this movement, but rather the beginning of the decolonisation of the university.'

They have already won their first battle, securing the removal of the Rhodes statue from UCT grounds in April 2015. Since then the student uprisings have morphed into the broader 'Fallist' movement, which has spread to other universities in South Africa and around the world. Its successor here has been the #FeesMustFall movement, launched in October 2015 to protest rising university fees in the country and to demand free quality and decolonised public education.

Irrespective of what the aims are of its various subgroups, the Fallist campaign continues to promote the 'fall' or rejection of 'white supremacy' as the foundation of its cause, and the embrace and promotion of 'black humanity' as its ultimate aim.

Well said.

It is only through large-scale redistribution that reconciliation and democracy can truly form the basis of our society and politics – when every South African citizen has obtained the 'better life' promised to them in 1994. Any discourse on nation building has to include fundamental redress of the dispossession that keeps black people impoverished, especially in relation to land and the economy. The 'rainbow nation' will remain a myth, a dream unfulfilled, if we do not alter the reality our people experience every day. Apartheid might have ended more than two decades ago, but we continue to suffer under a new black government, dominated by a new black elite who amass their wealth on the back of racial exploitation of the black poor, like the robber barons of yesteryear.

In order to get what we need from those who govern us, we have to know what exactly we are asking for. The narrative of decolonisation is the face of the current war being waged by many of our fellow citizens. But by questioning the legitimacy of an economic system that only perpetuates inequality, these students are also arguing against a more universal form of injustice.

The student resistance has ignited a debate of what it means to be free, challenging the notion that this country's revolution is complete. Now our youth are asking the same questions that those who fought apartheid once asked themselves. They want to know why their viewpoints have been defined by a Western model of knowledge which has trampled on equally important forms of indigenous wisdom in the past two millennia. They want to understand why their futures have been determined by a system that has built its foundations through conquest and theft; one that continues to threaten the global social fabric by exploiting nations and societies it regards as weaker or subordinate.

This narrative of decolonisation is the most powerful political analysis to emerge in the post-apartheid climate. It has destabilised the narrative of democracy and equality that was written at the dawn of the new South Africa, proving that transformation is hardly something that is achieved with a change of government, the writing of new laws or the drafting of a progressive constitution. These are only our tools. Now we need to begin using them.

Years of experience have taught me that the act of organising requires you to have a vision of where you want to be and a strategy for how to get there. Biko gave us the vision, the spark. But where is that spark today? And what is it?

We know that economic inequality and climate change are the greatest threats confronting humanity today, and how we choose to deal with them has repercussions for all species on this planet. Short of jumping into spaceships and fleeing to distant worlds, we need to change the way we are living now, here on earth.

It is not clear what image or concept will capture our imaginations and spur us on to start acting. Wealth inequality is an amorphous economic concept with an unemotive hook for many people desensitised to images of or statistics about the poor and hungry. Global warming is nearly impossible to grasp by many without scientific knowledge, or by climate-change denialists who fear confronting the reality of the world humans have created, and are destroying. But both are real, and both threaten our future.

I wonder where the Bikos of this generation are, the liberators who will unite a new group of activists around a common purpose. Perhaps it is not even necessary to wait for one, given that so many of us are still questioning what we stand for. There is no signature line defining the spirit of our struggle. There are no political martyrs or mavericks prepared to say, 'We are either for justice and freedom, or for apartheid and servitude.'

We need a spark, a lightning bolt. The embers of discontent burn, and sometimes they flare. But discontent alone cannot stop the rich and powerful from determining what kind of world we live in. The unhappiness of those suffering hardship, strife and marginalisation will not alter their reality.

The stakes are so high that we barely have time to contemplate what will happen if we keep going along the same route. It is undeniable that the future racing towards us is a horrifying one: a planet in ruins, destroyed in an ecological apocalypse that will bring wars and the deaths of billions.

But there is an alternative, a future in which human dignity, social justice and tolerance are prized. In this world humans live within our planetary boundaries and constantly search for new pathways of hope and opportunity for our children.

We need to find the spark that will help us build the foundations of this future. Perhaps the answer lies in the past, in the lessons and values that helped kick off one of history's most significant victories: the revolution that ended apartheid.

4

The Explosion

S o there was the spark, when I took those first tentative steps on the foothills of the mountain.

And yet I was not alone in venturing towards these heights of freedom. In the early 1970s tens of thousands of young South Africans were attempting the same thing, trying to figure out how to bring change to untenable circumstances.

Steve Biko lit up our collective consciousness and ignited our anger at the tyrannical apartheid regime. It was evident that something had to happen, and that it would happen soon.

The anger I felt during this time was not only on a collective level, shared with my fellow activists. It was deeply personal. Living in a city dominated by so-called liberal English whites had been worse for me than living with outright bigotry. I find being patronised insufferably worse than blunt racism. The daily assault of petty racist laws began to take its toll too. It was bitterly ironic that I, as a South African of Indian descent, was not even allowed to walk on the best beaches of the Indian Ocean unless I was a municipal worker cleaning up the mess left behind by whites.

This was the grand design of the regime, to deliberately and systematically dispossess the black majority of its most basic rights and civil liberties. Its hegemonic model of government was underlined by the destruction of indigenous culture and knowledge systems, which infiltrated every aspect of life for African workers. The onslaught of degradation they experienced seemed endless: low wages, the humiliation of the pass laws, the hardship of migrant labour and the hell of forced removals. It caused their sense of injustice to run even deeper than mine.

In my hometown of Durban, the growing unrest among the black population was expressed in a strike by African workers at the Coronation Brick and Tile factory which began on 9 January 1973. By the end of March over 100 000 workers had joined the protest, roughly half of the African working population in the biggest port city on the east coast.

The raw energy of the workers' struggle made a deep impression on my teenage mind. I was just out of high school and had no idea what I was going to do with my life, angry at the limited amount of career opportunities that were available to me as a South African of Indian descent. Apartheid had confined me to an existence that allowed me to perceive situations only from a racial viewpoint. But despite not having suffered the kind of injustice that African workers had experienced, there was something about their plight that resonated with me. The course of their lives was determined by what colour they were born, and yet they refused to accept it. This was when it occurred to me that I did not have to accept it either.

I felt a spark in my mind being lit again, as it had once been lit by Biko. But this time, I knew I had found the fuel to turn it into a full-blown explosion.

What I did not know was that the real explosion was yet to come.

I was lucky to be in the picture when the struggle finally erupted into an explosion. The modern-day fight against subjugation in South Africa was already centuries old when the turning point occurred, and before this there was no real knowing when that defining moment in the revolution would happen.

There is also ambiguity surrounding what exactly makes an event a turning point. How do we know an explosion when we see one? Sometimes what seems to be a life-changing event is nothing more than the temporary hollow roar of a dummy grenade, not the earth-shattering explosion we were hoping for.

On 21 March 1960, when 7 000 people gathered outside a police station in Sharpeville, a township near Johannesburg to contest the hated pass laws, there was no indication that the occasion would set off a new era of resistance politics in South Africa.

The protest, organised by the Pan Africanist Congress (PAC), seemed at first to be one of numerous peaceful protests and campaigns that were planned for that year to dispute the *dompas*. The police, however, seemed threatened by this picture of a unified black force demonstrating against a clearly unjust law. In a vicious and almost inconceivable move, they began firing at the protestors, who fled in all directions to escape the barrage of bullets assailing them. Sixty-nine people were killed, many shot in the back while they were retreating from the police.

The response of Hendrik Verwoerd's government to the massacre was swift and intense. A state of emergency was declared and 18 000 black people throughout the country were arrested. The ANC, PAC and all other resistance parties were banned, and prominent activists such as Nelson Mandela were declared terrorists, to be arrested on sight in what became the fully militarised apartheid state.

So does Sharpeville count as an explosion? Yes, because it set South Africa on an inevitable path to freedom. It had far-reaching consequences for the anti-apartheid movement, drawing outrage from the international community and bringing the tyrannical rule of the regime to the forefront of the world's political stage. But while Sharpeville helped to rally the black population into intensifying their campaign against the government, both the protest itself and its consequences were not enough to effect complete transformation. None of the pass laws were revoked, and the government displayed no repentance for its brutal display of power on unarmed civilians. Sixteen years later, when the Soweto uprising took place, the regime had perfected its ability to put down any form of resistance by the black majority.

The student protests on 16 June 1976 were sparked by the implementation of Afrikaans in black schools as a medium of instruction. Afrikaans was a language with which most black children were unfamiliar, and this was just another attempt by the regime to deny black people their basic rights, including a proper education. For many of these students, however, 'the language of the oppressor in the mouths of the oppressed' was a step too far. The strike, organised by the Soweto Students' Representative Council Action Committee, saw 20 000 students gathered outside Orlando West Secondary School to give voice to their anger in a language of their choice – one of solidarity and outrage.

The apartheid dispensation's response to this show of autonomy by a new generation of activists was to have its police fire their weapons at them. A thirteen-year-old boy named Hector Pieterson was caught in the crossfire, the picture of his lifeless body being carried by a fellow demonstrator becoming a powerful symbol of our resistance.

Instead of leaving us fearful or cowering, the government's increasingly violent treatment of those who dared to oppose apartheid only gave our movement more of the impetus it needed. There was no doubt in our minds that our cause was just, and that the rule of law in the land, which was discriminatory and entirely unjust, had to be vanquished.

What is more, this felt like the right moment to do so. It is difficult to describe, but the revolutionary fever that pulsed through us in this period – whether we were gathered in the dark of night plotting our next demonstration, or out on the streets protesting for our rights as students – was electrifying.

At the time I was a second-year student at the University of

Durban-Westville (now part of the University of KwaZulu-Natal) studying medicine, but my anger at what my fellow students had suffered in Soweto took up all my attention. Our rage seemed to be pumping through our blood at the same time, almost as if we were all tethered to one heart. We might have been young and still at school, but the protests were driven by us, the students, and we felt we had the support of the country's entire black population, as well as that of the planet. Anyone with a conscience or sense of justice had to agree with our fight for quality education, after all. Surely this would be enough to drive our movement towards victory?

It turns out organising is a little more complicated than that.

In retrospect the Soweto uprising of 1976 was a classic revolutionary movement. While the tension had been building for years, even centuries, the student protest was sparked by a single issue – a rejection of Afrikaans as a medium of instruction.

The anger that sent thousands of students into the streets was a focused one, and the tragedies that unfolded were very real, helping to put a human face on the struggles of a large group of people and to bring it into the larger context of anti-apartheid resistance. It is clear that this rage still smoulders among the country's students today. Former Afrikaans universities have a long way to go to eradicate the vestiges of an educational system that used race to deny black students the right to be taught in languages they understand.

The fact that race remains an obstacle in the growth of black education in South Africa is a testament to some of the failures of the past and the battles that were lost by the previous generation of student protestors. When we turned around and looked back on our struggle, we realised with stark clarity that there was no real organisation backing us up.

We might have believed ourselves victorious by revolting against the system, but we had not brought it down. We came to realise that struggle and transition are always more complex than initially assumed.

There was something missing. Our struggles were not effective, our voices were not being heard. It seemed we had not been asking ourselves the right questions.

It was only when Biko died the following year, in 1977, that I realised the obvious. Throughout our struggle we had been directing our rage *outwards*, towards the regime. What we should have been doing simultaneously was harnessing it *inwards*, by encouraging the people who shared our values to join us in our fight. There was no organised presence of academics, teachers, women, the rural community, workers or parents who were part of our movement. They understood our anger. It was their children who were being deprived of a worthwhile education and getting killed for demanding one. But what could they do? They had no impetus to help us stand up against the system, and we never provided them with any. They stood beside us as individuals, but individual bravery alone cannot defeat a ruthless armed enemy.

This is why we as students should have transformed the Afrikaans issue into something bigger, into a mobilising charter of demands linked to other, broader struggles.

We needed to organise, not only against the regime, but also around our exclusion and oppression. Because if a spark is to create an explosion that changes the world, the fuse must be an issue that resonates with the majority.

It was enormously painful for me to come to terms with this fact. In the terrible, tragic days following the uprising and Biko's death, I learnt that building a powerful, lasting movement entailed structuring it around issues that a plurality of people found important. Our collective rage as students was completely justified, but it was narrow. Unless a student uprising convinced the wider population of their shared grievances, it would always fail. We had to build a more welcoming, all-encompassing inclusive tent, and invite a bigger congregation to join us.

I remember experiencing that same feeling while visiting Cairo,

Egypt, months after the momentous Tahrir Square uprising in early 2011. Whenever I visited the city's cafés, university lecture halls or newly taken-over government buildings, I could sense the excitement of the citizens – students, intellectuals, women, workers – as they contemplated what lay ahead for their country. It was tangible, a kind of euphoria that I had experienced in my own youth.

But I also felt trepidation at the knowledge that this event, while ground-breaking, was just another cog in the ever-revolving wheel of revolutionary history. A history I know very well. I tried my best to brush my concerns away, but they lingered throughout my journey.

As a member of the advisory committee for the World Bank's Development Report on Conflict, Security and Development in 2011, I spent hours with Egypt's union leaders who wanted to free themselves from the previous 'conveyor belt' approach to unionism that had corrupted the union movement. They argued earnestly for an independent model that would never again be controlled by the state's security apparatus and political elites. But when I suggested a model that involved strong national industrial unions in a tight federation, similar to South Africa's COSATU, they baulked. In their view, a localised organisation of their unions, located on a factory-by-factory basis, was preferable because it would impede the state's ability to manipulate and undermine union leadership, as it had done pre-revolution.

I feel frustrated that my work in the region studying aspects of failed statehood prevented me from doing more. I could have offered a steady hand; I could have stood in solidarity with the unionists and youth when they needed people like me most. There was no one to share with them a progressive model of an independent union and collective bargaining. Today we know that their revolution failed because there was no consolidation of people's power, no constant working and reworking of democratic practices by the activists.

The uprisings that occurred in North Africa and the Middle

East in 2011 can be viewed as youth-led rebellions not only against entrenched privilege, but also against a social and political system that excludes the majority of its citizens from much-needed and rightful opportunities.

The years following the protests have been full of disappointments. Repression and torture have been restored to state rule. And yet for the young people in these regions who had a brief taste of liberation and human dignity, there can be no return to a faith in the old certainties and dogmas that stifled social and political progress for decades.

Meanwhile, the bright and talented youth on our continent are immigrating to the developed world or are trapped in tribal fiefdoms ruled by warlords. Some of the poorest risk their lives in their thousands to cross the Mediterranean in leaking boats, a large portion never reaching their destinations.

But there is still hope. The transformative wave fuelled by the frustration of our youth remains charged with energy and potential. They must now show enough initiative and discipline to pursue their goals if we are not to end up with another failed revolution.

When the end of apartheid arrived, it was not because of the accomplishments of student activists, who failed to fully utilise the explosive atmosphere of the Soweto uprising. Organising a massive movement centred on a common goal proved to be more complex than we ever realised.

So we were not part of that vanguard movement that brought overall change to South African politics. At best, we were a catalyst in creating the conditions that allowed the vanguard movement in organisations like the ANC to thrive. I came to learn this the hard way. Ultimately, it was Mandela's generation that provided us with the political project of our time – the goal of a constitutional democracy at the heart of which sits a commitment to social justice and the restoration of human dignity. That is what his movement promised the people, and that is what he delivered.

Despite all efforts, much of that proud legacy has been tainted by the current leadership in South Africa. Their rule of the country is underscored by a fatal ahistorical conceit that presumes past errors cannot be repeated and that the struggle for freedom cannot be un-won. This has been the most destructive oversight of the previous generation of activists – their belief that the fight for justice and equality was over in 1994. In fact, it had only begun. This is why I am making it my duty to share some of the lessons I have learnt from past mistakes with the current generation of leaders. Perhaps by doing this, I will add my own small contribution to the kind of future I hope they will build, and which I and my compatriots could not.

5

Organise or Starve

THIS IS THE story of how I got it wrong before I got it right. In the immediate aftermath of the Soweto uprising I was frustrated and angry, the fuse of my activism doused. I took stock of who and what surrounded me, wondering what my next step should be. It was now clear that if we as students were to achieve anything, our struggle had to include a mass of people behind it. We had to think and act differently.

But I was unsure of how to help initiate community involvement in the anti-apartheid movement. I had always felt tremendous solidarity and a deep connection with workers, the human cogs in hyper-industrial apartheid South Africa's corporate machinery. Without their sweat and labour, the white state would never have attained the wealth and resources that allowed it to sustain its racist rule of the country.

In 1973 I was fortunate to witness militant labourers marching through the streets of Durban, protesting the inhuman conditions in which they were forced to work. I felt the raw rage of their cause and it empowered me, a fellow black South African, to see their defiance in the face of intimidation – even when it involved batons, bullets, dogs and tear gas. Through such actions, the workers proved they were an army ready to be organised.

After 1976 South African students were also in a full-on war with the regime. Every vocal student organisation in the country had been banned, and the police were ruthless in their persecution of the most politically active among us. At one point my mother was even called in by the security police to answer questions about my activities at the SASO branch of the University of Durban-Westville where I was studying. Hundreds of my comrades were living under similar circumstances, some paying the ultimate price for standing up to the regime. I soon became accustomed to attending underground funerals.

With Biko dead, many black consciousness adherents were searching for other meaningful interpretations of activists' roles in a tyrannical state that privileges one group over another.

In a police state we wolfed down revolutionary literature from a number of political and militant authors, including Lenin's *What is to be Done? Burning Questions of Our Movement*, which analyses the weaknesses of student activism and convinced me of the gains of building a militant working-class movement; as well as Paulo Freire's *Pedagogy of the Oppressed*, which spelled out the importance of literacy in mass social movements. Other stand-out readings of this time were Sun Tzu's *The Art of War*, Crane Brinton's *The Anatomy of Revolution* and Frantz Fanon's *The Wretched of the Earth*. We studied the ideas of nationalist or Marxist theorists such as Thomas Sankara, Antonio Gramsci and Amílcar Cabral. Our motivation for turning to these scholars was a human one. We were searching for a connection, a sense of kinship. Surely others elsewhere in the world had confronted the challenges that South Africans under apartheid experienced every day.

They most certainly had. The theory of change and the science of revolution have been extensively studied for centuries. Discontent was widespread, as indicated in the movements opposing the Vietnam War of the previous decade. Then as now, people around the world were subject to the inequalities wrought by a small political and wealthy elite.

But it was when I read Rick Turner's *The Eye of the Needle: Towards Participatory Democracy in South Africa* that I discovered my calling as an activist for the independent worker movement.

Turner, along with his friend Steve Biko, was a leading figure in the Durban Moment, that turbulent period in the early 1970s when the city was a hotbed of political activism. A prominent academic at the University of Natal, Turner supported the growth of independent trade unionism underpinned by activism and the principle of workers' control. For him, popular democracy had to be built from below, free from the constraints of authoritarian strands of thought such as those found in the leftist Stalinist movement and partisan politics. His interest in workers' rights led him to participate in the wages commissions of the National Union of South African Students (NUSAS) from 1971 to 1973, when he helped investigate the working conditions of African workers.

Turner was assassinated on 8 January 1978, shot through the window of his home in the Durban suburb of Bellair. His killers were never found, but it is believed that apartheid security forces had a hand in his murder. Like Biko's death the previous year, the loss of Turner left a void in the ideology of many student and youth movements in the country. We were searching for the missing link in the story of exploitation that lay at the heart of the racist system.

In the Black Consciousness Movement, divergences in thinking began to arise between an increasingly radical and class-orientated SASO and its umbrella organisation, the Black People's Convention (BPC). I never joined the BPC because they had strong anti-communist leanings with which I could not agree.

But for most of us socialism was the philosophy we believed could lift us out of the exclusionary binds of apartheid ideology. There was something appealing about the socialist grand vision of egalitarianism and its all-encompassing conviction that history was the 'record of class struggles'. As socialists, our goal was to eradicate the system of racial capitalism in its entirety, not just deracialise it.

We began to debate, quite fiercely at times, which direction we were to take in the wake of the Soweto uprising. I spoke strongly of my intention to join a fledgling union movement of black workers, but I was challenged on this front by certain members who were also part of the ANC underground. They believed this approach was too reformist because negotiations with employers through unions would supposedly blunt the militancy of the working class. To obtain access to the workers, I would also have to work in a system that was prescribed by the apartheid regime.

I chose to ignore these arguments. It was my strong belief that to conquer apartheid injustices, I had to work with the people most affected by them – black labourers.

As I soon found out, factories were the perfect place to start. And back then, to work in a factory or mine in South Africa was a nightmare. They formed the very nexus of exploitation. Black people, often migrant workers, were sucked towards the factories and mines for cheap labour and paid starvation wages. They faced arbitrary dismissals, bad health and safety conditions, and over-crowded workplaces. And yet while women were denied maternity rights and all workers a pension fund, the white bosses became fantastically rich. These owners naturally had ties to the regime, conspiring with it to quash any attempts by workers to obtain better wages. Strikes were usually met with a heavy police presence aimed at intimidating the workers.

Ours was by no means the first generation of South Africans to try to unite workers into an effective and enduring movement.[1] Nor were the workers passive and submissive individuals who waited, sheep-like, for something to be done on their behalf. When the strike at Coronation Brick in Durban occurred in January 1973 I had watched as workers marched down Durban's streets demanding change, and without inciting any violence. After more than 100 000 workers joined the strike, the factories were forced to give in and labourers won the salary increases they had been asking for.

The win might not have been big, but it was a win nonetheless. And now I would be joining their cause after years of being a student and community activist. I found the highly repetitive and stagnant elements of student protest exhausting, and I was eager to use what I had learnt from it in a movement that could actually help black people. I knew much about strategy and tactics, which would also come in handy during negotiations. I believed I was more than ready for this new challenge.

It was late 1979 when I received my first union assignment. I was twenty-five and would be working as a volunteer for the Federation of South African Trade Unions (FOSATU) to help rehabilitate its moribund sweet workers' branch.

FOSATU carried out its strategies smartly, using a long history of international union organisation as its guide and adapting it to a South African context. The theories of Marxist intellectuals and academics like Rick Turner also influenced its outlook, particularly in the distinction they drew between tactics and principle, which are intricately linked.

There was a lot for me to learn, however, especially about the nature of labour unions and what their real purpose is. At its heart, a union's primary objective is to increase the bargaining power of workers by organising them as a collective with the same aims. If workers are united and can speak with one voice, management has no choice but to listen to what they have to say. Or so the reasoning goes. Unions present workers' interests and concerns to management, and lobby the government to provide better protection for workers' rights through regulation. In this can be seen the vital role unions can play in organising almost any movement, anywhere in the world.

When I began volunteering I already knew what labour unions had done to advance workers' rights and to change the very fabric of society. It was labour unions that drove the struggle for justice and human dignity in the earliest stages of the Industrial Revolution in Britain and Europe. Through their efforts, and often bloody struggles, the exploitative practices of the oppressive industrial class were put to task and rights were won that helped make the world a fairer place. Labourers at this time worked in wretched conditions, earning dismal wages with very little leisure time, and many were children. In apartheid South Africa, many mine, factory and farm labourers worked in similar conditions.

I learnt that strong shop-floor organisation was key to liberating factory workers from inequity in the workplace. Shop stewards, empowered with the right legal, negotiating and communication skills, formed the backbone of the movement. Their participation contributed to a democratic structure that emphasised the principle of workers' control and made worker delegates the majority in all parts of the federation.

I embraced this notion of building a membership-based organisation that placed control of union resources in workers' hands. While we did raise funds from our partners in Scandinavia, Netherlands and Canada, all of whom were very supportive of us, we made sure not to be dependent on a donor-driven model that would ultimately undermine our independence. We made sure that our organisation could function by itself, without outside support, by getting the workers themselves to sustain it.

This was long before the days of stop-order deductions. Union dues were collected by hand and a receipt was issued to the worker. We never had to worry about union representatives stealing from workers as every cent was accounted for. Worker-controlled structures oversaw all income and expenditure at every level. As union officials, we were driven by the spirit of volunteerism and service, and had no inclination to engage in corrupt practices that would only undermine our efforts at improving workers' lives.

The principle of negotiations was based on mandates and report-backs. It was unheard of for leaders to meet in secret with management, and delegates from every factory could participate in the discussions. Bargaining was done collectively, which made it imperative for us to build a national industrial union to increase our numbers and create a powerful national movement.

And while the modern trade union movement in South Africa was full of potential activists ready for recruitment into the ANC and the struggle, FOSATU was cautious about allying itself with any political or community organisations. Among our ranks were key white Marxist strategists who harboured ambitions of an independent workers' party that would form an alternative to the South African Communist Party (SACP), which they viewed as Stalinist and bureaucratic. In particular, they took issue with the party's hold over unions that required SACP affiliation from workers if they wanted to be members. This reflected how unionism worked in the past, when it was mainly seen as an extension of political organisations, and which resulted in the weakening of unions' initial prerogatives for their workers.

Like many union officials, I was attracted to the ANC because it had a well-established leadership and its alliance with the SACP bolstered its reputation as a party that incorporated class analysis in its ethos. But I learnt never to force ANC ideology down the throats of union members. The backbone of the modern union movement consisted of migrant workers who lived a brutal existence in prisoner dormitories and hostels. It was not necessary for me to stand on a soapbox and tell them what was wrong with our society. They already lived it. Union leaders understood that by building workplace democracy, the political consciousness of our members and their confidence in the working class would automatically rise in tandem. In fact, I soon came to realise that I could learn a lot more about the struggle from the union workers than they could learn from me. Their courage and wisdom have given me some of my most cherished and enduring life lessons.

If all this sounds complicated, that is because it cannot be simple. There are no shortcuts to organising and especially building unions. Usually, when I describe my union days to people unfamiliar with how such organisations work, they seem baffled by the complexity.

So was I, for many years.

When I did learn, it was the hard way. And that's a good thing. Difficult lessons made a greater impact on me than those that came easily to me.

Back then, even getting to locations to carry out union work required a lot of energy. Every morning I woke up hours before sunrise and jumped into a borrowed Volkswagen to get to the Beacon Sweets factory in Durban before 4 a.m. Then I would stand in front of the building like some crazed apparition that somehow always made its appearance at the darkest time of the morning, trying to solicit workers to join the union.

'Do you want to get me fired?' they used to ask me when I approached them, motivational speech at the ready. It was a valid question. Factory management had been keeping an eye on the skinny Indian guy with the slogans and communist literature for some time, and my presence endangered the workers starting or ending their shifts.

But I was adamant to keep trying to recruit workers, even though they saw me as poisonous. My efforts in this regard were largely futile, however.

On one cold lonely morning, as I made another fruitless effort to sign up a few workers, an older man, who seemed to have something on his mind, approached me and said, 'Hey, sonny boy. Come with me.'

Too embarrassed to continue beseeching workers who could not take me seriously, I decided to follow him. We walked some distance until we were out of sight of the factory gates.

The man then proceeded to critique my performance outside the factory. He wasn't very complimentary.

'No one understands your pamphlets,' he explained to me. 'And if workers are seen talking to you outside the factory gate, they will be harassed by management who are monitoring you.'

He made it clear that forcing my presence on workers right outside the factory was the dumbest way possible to solicit interest in the union, and he gave me a few other suggestions for getting the workers to listen to me. All of them were brilliant.

Instead of parading myself in front of the factory, drawing unnecessary attention to both myself and the workers, the old man advised that I go to their homes to speak to them. In such intimate settings we would be outside the gaze of management's all-seeing eye. He suggested as well that I ask the workers questions, not just offer them answers. To find out what the workers wanted, I needed to have a conversation with them, not lecture them. This was their union, after all. If it was going to be successful, I had to build it with them, by their side.

At first, it was not easy for me to hear this. But my dedication to the union was genuine, and I had to swallow my pride if I wanted to know how to help the workers. The years have wiped the name and face of the old man from my memory, but the advice he gave me that day has stayed with me forever. He was one of many guides who passed on their wisdom to me during my work as a union representative. I am eternally grateful to him.

Following that fateful conversation, I made a fervent effort to start listening to what the workers had to say. I made sure that I did not just talk at them.

And it worked.

I began by taking a job as a labourer in a textile mill to understand the kind of hardships factory workers faced every day. I also needed to know what limitations existed inside a factory – the contradictions, conflicts and challenges – that would inhibit organisation. The goal was always to create unity, even in the ranks of the oppressed.

It was only by literally walking in their footsteps that I could begin to understand what it was like for workers on the factory floor and what it was they needed from me. These were the people who formed the majority of South Africa's working poor, so I had to speak to them about *their* wants and *their* needs. I finally understood that attaining their trust, and their mandate, required union officials to *hear* them first. This is a key lesson of activism. Immersing ourselves in the experiences of the people we represent and understanding the adversities they face is crucial for knowing how to speak about their interests.

Only after this were we able to begin negotiating with other organisations and labour movements – those of miners, steelworkers and plumbers – because we had an idea of what their constituents were going through. With these new players on our side, we forged an even broader consensus for workers' rights.

Pole, pole.

It took some time, but I was finally figuring out what it takes to organise workers.

Like most activists at the time, Marx was my reading matter. We found truth in his argument that a vanguard movement must lead an organised working class in order to socialise the means of production, thus laying the basis for a classless society. Working from this, I could see a militant, politicised union movement developing at the point of production and spearheading the struggle for scientific socialism. My contemporaries shared this view, committing their heart and soul to this cause. Many of the fundamental privileges in the workplace that we take for granted today originated in the gigantic battles waged by unions for the eight-hour day, health and social security, and broader democratic rights in society.

For unions to carry out such feats, they have to create consensus among their various constituents.

Of course, this sounds easier than it is. Put one hundred people in a room and you will hear one hundred points of view.

But let's say you have already canvassed these people and established a baseline of their concerns. Doing this not only allows you to understand the issues that are of paramount importance to them, but to formulate a plan that will keep your members happy. Now you have a common base to work from, which will give you a fighting chance at establishing consensus.

This was a key lesson for me in my earliest days as a labour organiser. I had to shut my mouth and learn what was best. The workers were dirt poor, but they were not victims. They showed such resilience in adversity that it was sometimes hard for me to believe it. They did not need pamphlets to explain to them what they wanted. They already knew.

As the wise old man had shown me, the workers needed something different from the unions than what I was offering. I had seen the union as a springboard from which to free the country from apartheid and right the wrongs of 1976. But the most important concern for the workers was obtaining enough job security so that they could continue feeding themselves and their families. They wanted dignity on the shop floor and to be treated like humans, not beasts.

I got working. I spoke to the workers about how I had committed class suicide, abandoning the comfort and even privilege of my former place in the lower middle class. I went to peoples' homes, met their families and ate with them. They had very little, but what little they had they shared with me. I had *shisa nyama*, or barbecued meat, in the hostels with the migrant workers, sharing stories, laughing and planning our next steps.

That sense of camaraderie is missing today in union interactions with their members. I don't see union officials breaking cultural, class and language barriers like we did in our dealings with labourers. Such moments, for me, led to the birth of my identity. I might have been Indian in origin, but my race was never an issue for the African people I met and worked with. I did not feel I belonged to a racial grouping in the apartheid scheme of things. I never did, and never will, allow others to classify me on any basis. It was enough for me that the workers treated me with respect, and that I did the same for them. I was always their comrade, and this knowledge is what fired my passion for the movement every day. I listened, I learned, and I slowly began to gain momentum in bringing new members into the fold. *I realised that we were building a family.*

Around the country there were others, irrespective of the colour of their skin, who were doing the same thing. Thousands of activists like me were committing themselves to the revolutionary act of organising a movement. The air was palpable with expectation. It was clear that something remarkable was happening. The harder union organisers worked and the more we listened, the greater the respect and trust from those we recruited. Older workers, who had been active in politics and unions in their youth, now streamed into our ranks, finding hope in what we were standing for even after decades of repression and false starts.

Suddenly, the labour movement was an organisation. Events and opportunities would occur without our input, initiative or guidance. By themselves, members were choosing to organise in other factories, dedicating themselves to our cause. Our message was spreading among labourers as they travelled together on trains, or met at church or the shebeen. Soon the cause of the union was no longer the prerogative of only union officials. It formed the basis of a genuine workers' movement. Members had become leaders in their communities, identifying their fight for labour rights with the struggles of local and political leaders, as well as with students protesting the use of Afrikaans in schools.

Things were changing.

And when new events are inspired by mass action and an ideology that prizes the needs of the many, it becomes extremely hard to unchange these events.

Those of us fighting the system were now scaling our own

Kilimanjaro. It was a brutal, seemingly impossible task, but some-thing was telling me we were making real progress. And although I could see higher peaks in the distance, I also knew that the summit lay beyond.

6

The Objective Objective

M Y YEARS OF experience as a union leader and community activist have led many people to ask me for advice on organising. While I cannot claim to be an authority on social action, I have learnt many lessons which I am willing to share with activists to help them get started. In many of my interactions, the concern that seems to consume fledgling community leaders most is also a question I have often asked myself during my own journey.

Is there a difference between organising for good and organising for evil?

The answer might seem obvious, but this is a deeply relevant question in the modern political climate, where it has become increasingly hard to tell the difference between the good guys and the bad guys. And in unions or organisations where so many varied opinions can exist, one man's good can easily be another woman's evil.

But I learnt early in my union journey that there are objective ways to judge the effect of a movement's actions on those they believe to be defending, as well as on the groups or people they are opposed to. As there are in any huge undertaking, caveats exist that help activists determine whether their movements will be successes or failures, and how they will be depicted in the annals of history.

Of course, the number of qualifications attached to your cause depends entirely on what you are working towards, and the ultimate aims of your movement. It should be plain by now that none of these limitations are to be placed on obtaining the best possible result for the people you are representing.

One of the abiding ironies of apartheid rule was how easily the regime labelled those fighting against it as 'terrorists'. History has shown that neither the ANC nor its military wing, Umkhonto we Sizwe (MK), engaged in indiscriminate violence as a political strategy. As leaders of the ANC, both Nelson Mandela and Oliver Tambo were willing to use force, but only as an extension of their political aims. They were always mindful of the dangers of using violence to fight a violent enemy, determined not to become like their oppressors, who felt no qualms about the harm they inflicted on so many people.

Branding anti-apartheid activists terrorists was an insidious tactic by the white government to maintain its authoritarian power over black South Africans. It was the apartheid regime that was perpetrating its own brand of terror on the majority of the country's population. But by proliferating the lie that resistance groups were hostile communists, they provided the white population and Western politicians, engaged in the Cold War, with a valid reason for their continuing suppression of blacks in the country. Apartheid hard-liners had carte blanche to treat us as agitators and enemies of the state. We became legitimate targets of covert hit squads and sponsored assassins. In fact, Mandela's capture before his imprisonment was the result of a collaboration between the United States' Central Intelligence Agency and apartheid security forces to destabilise any organisation that was not allied to America's national security goal of defeating communism.

Those of us in the labour movement were also at risk of being named traitors of the state. As leaders in a mass movement, we were under constant surveillance, and COSATU, a militant organisation, generally always walked that fine line between the legal and the illegal.

But there was a crucial difference between our reasons for using force and those of the apartheid government. The latter regularly employed the police force and army to violently put down individuals they considered enemies, or to subdue large numbers of people engaged in peaceful protests – even if these protestors were children as June 16 proved. The ANC, however, along with its militant branch MK, was united around a vision of freedom for *all* South Africans. The Freedom Charter, adopted at the Congress of the People on 26 June 1955, fully laid out the objective of the anti-apartheid movement to restore human rights to every person in the country. Our armed struggle was our means of defending our people against a regime that criminalised our protests and stole our birth rights: 'We, the People of South Africa, declare for all our country and the world to know: that South Africa belongs to all who live in it, black and white, and that no government can justly claim authority unless it is based on the will of all the people.'

This was the vision underlining the ANC's strategy for creating a new South Africa, built around the simple core demand of 'one person, one vote, in a free, democratic, non-sexist, non-racial South Africa'.

As the anti-apartheid movement garnered the attention of international social justice institutions and organisations, activists in South Africa began directing their focus on the principle of people-to-people solidarity.

By this, I mean that we actually worked with the people we were representing. We were not like those non-governmental organisations that claim to be functioning on behalf of people suffering injustice, disease and poverty, but when it comes to implementing a charitable programme, they let donors and bilateral aid agencies decide the parameters for doing so.

When I hear discussions about organising today, I often feel conflicted. The whole business reminds me of those moments I experienced as a child looking through a fence while white children laughed and shrieked on merry-go-rounds. 'Why can't I go on the horses?' I used to ask my parents. They would only bow their heads in response, possibly in shame.

The industrial development complex is like the merry-go-rounds of my past – meant to bring contentment to all individuals, but reserved only for a select few. In a business context, those with access to the funds are usually acting on behalf of rich donors who dispense favours based on how these will benefit them most. Even where there is noble intention, a need for funding creates high recurrent cost models and distorts remuneration dynamics. The result is an arrogant bureaucracy increasingly alienated from its cause and primary support base.

It must be understood that donors, the media and governments are not the shareholders of civil society. The people are.

Those of us fighting in the struggle had to search for other allies for our organisations since most Western leaders had no interest in our plight. Bypassing heads of state and appealing directly to overseas trade unions, student movements and churches, we earned massive political, moral and financial support. And it was only when citizens outside of South Africa put pressure on their leaders to do something about apartheid that leaders like Margaret Thatcher and Ronald Reagan finally imposed sanctions on South Africa in the eighties.

Now the current generation of leaders needs to circumvent well-resourced and powerful institutions that exclude the majority from their rightful access to the country's wealth. Young activists need to win the support of the public – of parents, workers, and the urban and rural populace – to help them take back power from the powerful. The only dream for many of these people is for a better life for their children than they had. They do not regard the youth's burning down of libraries, lecture theatres, schools and community facilities as appropriate actions to obtain what is rightfully theirs. Such manoeuvres merely play into the hands of institutions – particularly those of the state – seeking to demonise activism on all fronts and repress any challenges to their authority.

My journey as a union organiser taught me that *the goal is to unite our people, build workers' power and catalyse leadership at grassroots level.* This kind of approach considers the needs of every person who has cause for complaint and enables negotiations on issues that affect our members directly. It prevents the intrusion of personal agendas on community movements and development, ensuring that the needs of the people, before anything else, take precedence. There is not, and never will be, place for a 'big chief' in any democratic organisation.

We live in a world in which individual success is feted. Where being poor is the fault of the person, not the system. These are the central tenets of the dominant world religion known as neoliberalism. What it advocates is a laissez-faire form of liberalism, the kind of economic policy that eliminates price controls, deregulates markets, propagates free trade, and diminishes state influence on the economy through privatisation and fiscal austerity.

Neoliberalism formed the underlying philosophy of both Thatcher's and Reagan's governments in the eighties. These politicians prioritised the role of the private sector, allowing total freedom of movement for capital, goods and services in a way that strengthened the stranglehold of transnationals on our economies and globalised our national elites.

We were all supposed to be the beneficiaries of such trickle-down economics as an unregulated market should, in theory, be the primary source of a country's jobs. Instead, this system rejects government regulation of the market, assigning all control of money supply to banks. The interests of consumers, who sustain the system, are overlooked, while the capitalist aims of the tiny elite at the top of the food chain are given unlimited scope.

These principles are the foundations of the current world order of disposable consumption, embraced by policymakers because of the unlimited stream of wealth it pumps into business and government. Ever-increasing growth and production sustain the consumerist mindset, presupposing an infinite supply of planetary resources. The outcome has been the super-exploitation of our natural and mineral resources and the current ecological crisis of climate change. *A global financial system that places money before people and planet drives all international relations and intrudes on nearly every aspect of individual life.* Commodification has taken over our interactions with people, which depend on the clothes we wear, our phones, our cars, our consumer-driven lifestyles. The phenomenon of 'retail therapy', in the meantime, encourages con-sumerism even when we have no money to buy any goods.

The most prominent exponent of neoliberal theory was American economist Milton Friedman, who emphasised individual success before the interests of the collective. Those who are smarter than others or more talented are more entitled to wealth than those who have neither of these attributes, nor the means with which to utilise them. In this system, competitiveness between people and states is encouraged because the more you have, the more powerful you are. 'Is there some society you know that doesn't run on greed?' asks Friedman. 'You think Russia doesn't run on greed? You think China doesn't run on greed? What is greed? Of course, none of us are greedy; it's only the other fellow who's greedy. The world runs on individuals pursuing their separate interests.' The hope was that once individuals made enough money to assuage their greed, they would invest in production and create more jobs.

As an advisor to both Reagan and Thatcher in the 1980s, when the Soviet Union was in decline, Friedman exercised an enormous influence on the economic policies of two of the most powerful nations in the world. He helped create the monster of financial capitalism which overrode and dominated the older industrial and agricultural sectors. The various offshoots of his model, parading as business science, were then taught as gospel in universities and MBA schools of management around the world.

By the end of the 1980s neoliberals were arguing that socialism was dead. The fall of the Berlin Wall in 1989 signalled the massive defeat of Soviet-style communism, which had tarnished the egalitarian outlook advocated by socialism. In their excesses and corruption, the former vanguard leadership of the USSR's Communist Party proved to be no different from the rest of the world's predatory elites, exploiting their citizens and disregarding their humanity to serve only their own selfish ends.

Neoliberal philosophy is now seen as hegemonic and sacrosanct. Any divergent views on the role of the state, markets and people are marginalised and ridiculed as unrealistic, utopian and idealistic. This, even while power and wealth are increasingly concentrated in the hands of a few and societies are dominated by economic and political elites. In developing nations this system wreaks havoc on economies that are already short of resources and the growth of which is stunted by interference from organisations such as the World Bank and the IMF, which are controlled by powerful and wealthy countries in the West.

For a union leader like myself who had championed socialism as the groundwork for building a new society, the dawn of the neoliberal era naturally made a great impact on me. I had worked closely with communist leaders in South Africa who ranked as some of the most committed activists I had ever met, although I never joined the SACP because I would no doubt have had difficulty toeing the party line.

Still, I was desperate to understand what had brought about the governing crisis in the Soviet Union, determined that the movement I was part of in South Africa never made the same mistakes. In 1990, in my capacity as general secretary of COSATU, I led a delegation to the rapidly deteriorating and fragmented Red Empire. My conversations with the country's union leadership left me horrified. They were nothing more than adjuncts of the Communist Party leadership, playing no role whatsoever in determining socio-economic policy. I remember thinking that if COSATU leaders were trade unionists in the Soviet Union, we would certainly have ended up in the labour camps of Siberia.

The USSR provided further proof that governments invested with too much power can commit terrible atrocities. An overcompensation of authority allows political leaders to restrict the flow of wealth and opportunity to tiny groups of individuals or businesses, who then take advantage of these laws which harm the majority.

Apartheid was such a deeply unjust system of rule because it only served the country's white citizens. Whether you were part of South Africa's elite or underclass was based solely on the colour of your skin or your ethnicity. The white government, in the implementation of its racist agenda, never considered what the majority of the county's people wanted. They were well aware that tens of millions of people would never be complicit in their own subjugation. So to keep their racial and exclusionary policies in place, apartheid leaders employed violence to put down anyone who opposed them.

By not receiving a mandate from the majority of South Africa's citizens, apartheid was, in contrast to democracy, a corrupt, illegal form of rule; the only thing separating it from other illegitimate forms being how blatantly it enforced its unjust laws.

Compare this to the tyranny that the United States of America – held up by its citizens as a paradigm of modern freedom – inflicts on other nations it aims to control under the guise of democracy. The various draconian laws to which it subjects some of its own citizens, as well as sovereign nations over which it has no authority, undermine the validity of its self-appointed moniker as 'the land of the free'.

In 2003, without the sanction of the United Nations, and against the advice of numerous political and religious leaders, including Nelson Mandela and former archbishop Desmond Tutu, the US, in a coalition with the United Kingdom, manufactured evidence of weapons of mass destruction in Iraq and initiated a war that had more to do with the capture of strategic oil reserves than the restoration of democracy.

The human cost of this misguided war has made the world a less safe place for millions of Iraqis, with over half a million dead and many displaced. Thirteen years later, the Middle East remains in geopolitical turmoil despite the trillions of dollars the US has spent apparently clearing the region of 'terror'. Chaos persists in Syria and Afghanistan, as well as in African countries with large Muslim populations, such as Libya. It is soul-shattering to think of what could have been done with the money spent on that war. Instead of creating hatred, bridges of love, hope and compassion could have been built.

Terrorism cannot be defeated through wars and the destruction of stable nations and communities. The Iraq War ended up having a far-reaching impact on the rest of the world as well, affecting the lives of people globally. In the years following the World Trade Center attacks on 11 September 2001, the American government invested itself with the authority to strangle our freedom of speech and impose on our privacy by reading our emails and tapping our phones, as Edward Snowden eventually revealed to the world. In its 'war on terror', the US set out to arrest or torture anyone they suspected of being a terrorist, with or without evidence.

It is clear that regardless of the face they show to the world, both those who perpetrate terror and those who claim to fight it have one crucial thing in common. They do not work with, but against. They do not negotiate or ask, but order and impose. Instead of engaging with a local population and drawing up a framework for a functional, consensus-based democracy, they declare war on it.

Terrorism is the use of fear-inducing violence by an individual, group, institution or government to achieve some stated or explicit objective. Terrorists are not only sociopaths who live in caves in the desert.

Our governments, by virtue of their control over state resources such as security and law enforcement, have the power to utilise these resources to enforce organised violence. And similar to the reasons that extremists give for committing acts of terrorism, governments can also use violence and propaganda to advance their power both in their own countries and in others.

The rise of more blatant racism, sexism and xenophobia in world politics and international relations is one manifestation of this tactic in recent times.

In a world in which an inordinate number of people are without jobs or living in poverty, many are correct in blaming the establishment for their predicament. And in these fraught political contexts, right-wing demagogues have found it easy to take up the mantle of liberator and to promote a populist ideology that they claim will rid their countries of the scapegoats they choose to blame for their problems. Usually these are people of a different colour, or whose culture, language, religion or sexual orientation are anathema to their values. The Brexit win in the UK and Donald Trump's election as president of the United States, both occurring in 2016, are proof that polarisation in societies is deepening. Hate, fear and fundamentalism are the new demands of increasingly angry and bigoted voting publics struggling to come to terms with the diversity now defining their countries' populations.

The firebrands of this right-wing populism, the Trumps and Marine le Pens of this world, almost seem to thrill in the rage that consumes their voters, to relish inspiring some of the worst instincts of humanity and a renewed belief in the value of a fascist system of rule.

For socialists such as Trotsky, this kind of 'individual terror is inadmissible precisely because it belittles the role of the masses in their own consciousness, reconciles them to their powerlessness, and turns their eyes and hopes towards a great avenger and liberator who some day will come and accomplish his mission'.[1]

White supremacists, racist politicians and a biased media frequently expound the idea of a shared struggle to press forward their hateful agenda, many times inciting their followers or readers to kill or maim those they consider intruders. Although popular struggles against slavery, colonialism and other unjust systems have also invoked an armed component, these actions usually stemmed from a point of desperation, when all other avenues for change had been explored.

Mandela argued that the ANC's liberation movement against apartheid turned to violence because no other alternative existed after decades of peaceful demonstrations and appeals to the white government. However, as in any movement that employs violence to achieve its aims, there were innocent casualties in MK'S campaign against the state, and Mandela himself admitted that the ANC violated human rights on certain occasions during its struggle for equality. As leader of this party, he accepted responsibility for these errant isolated acts.[2]

Terrorists, in contrast, make no coherent political demands. What they desire is impractical or harmful – usually a return to a draconian adherence to a perverse form of religion, or the power to exploit natural and mineral resources. They perpetuate deliberate acts of mass murder with the primary goal of inflicting massive pain, suffering and devastation.

Extremist groups recruit by filling a political vacuum created by the systemic exclusion of an entire generation from education and social advancement. They present a stark picture of the enemy, particularly to young people, then they offer them an identity, a purpose, a future, a gun and even a salary. For the marginalised youth in war-torn countries, terror groups give them the opportunity to seek revenge on the oppressive elites living in luxury while their people starve. Terror organisations such as Boko Haram in northern Nigeria, Al-Shabaab in Somalia and the Islamic State in Syria have been able to swell their ranks because of widespread anger and discontent among the youth in their regions.

Of course, these groups, whether state-sponsored or not, are simply one more narrow elite seeking to displace another narrow elite. Boko Haram does not care about the ordinary citizens of northern Nigeria. The group's only concern is occupying the region's power vacuum and reaping the spoils. The same goes for the Islamic State, filling the gaps created by a dysfunctional rule of law in Iraq and Syria. Their work is next to easy.

Terrorists take anger and turn it into a weapon. They use coercion and violence to carry out their aims, creating enough chaos to replace one type of misery with another. They do not work towards solutions that can benefit the majority.

And yet there seems to be little difference between the kind of atrocities committed by the Islamic State and those of the Assad government in Syria; the actions of extremists like Norway's neo-Nazi Anders Behring Breivik, who killed seventy-seven people, most of them students, in July 2011, or the regular spate of school shootings in the United States, including the Sandy Hook shooting in December 2012, in which twenty children were killed.

While defenceless people are gunned down by deranged men with extreme ideas, black people continue to be the targets of racial profiling, systematic harassment and often fatal shootings by the police in countries like America and South Africa. The Marikana shootings on 16 August 2012 were the most brutal display of police violence against civilians in the country since Sharpeville, and presented a turning point in our democracy's history. In our government's choice to protect the commercial interests of a corrupt mining company instead of its struggling workers, the true extent of the state capture of our institutions was exposed. It was proof that elitism and the politics of a minority still determine the state's treatment of the marginalised in our society.

Atrocities against innocent individuals have become the norm on our planet, whether by security forces and armies employed by corrupt governments, or by extremist groups who kill indiscriminately. Too often the response has been to meet violence with more violence, filling the void of development and progress with death.

Those of us who are the potential victims of such acts, or who are outraged for those who are, need to unite in a comprehensive global campaign that will call for peace and an end to all wars. We have to start asking ourselves some hard questions. Who are the real terrorists and lords of war? Who are the individuals and what are the institutions enabling violence and terrorism in countries all over the world?

It is easy to only consider extremists as the main perpetrators of terrorism, but the arms industries in countries claiming to be the protectors of democracy also profit from this conflict. The military-industrial complex that provides guns and ammunition to despotic governments and extremist groups presents the main challenge to the establishment of peace in terror-affected countries. It has created a global nexus of corruption that embraces political institutions and determines electoral outcomes through party funding and lobbying in many arms-producing countries.

During the resistance against apartheid, I learnt painfully that the state is always better armed than its citizens. So in the continual battle for workers' rights, we at COSATU channelled the lessons that Sun Tzu espoused in his *Art of War* for winning our own struggle. We learnt that victory comes when you recognise when to attack and when to draw back; by sharing the same goals as your fellow fighters; by knowing the weaknesses of both your enemy and yourself; and through the capable leadership of a commander who has the mandate and support of his troops. These are also lessons for building non-violent mass action.

In the anti-apartheid struggle Nelson Mandela was our leader, the symbol of our resistance and the most famous and beloved prisoner in the world. He inspired all kinds of people with a sense of right to join the liberation effort and to unite around the goal of obtaining equal rights for all South Africans. There were opportunities to fight apartheid in small ways and big ways. People chose to buy oranges from Spain instead of South Africa; foreign students mobilised their universities to disinvest from the country; church leaders appealed to their congregations to speak out against the immorality of apartheid; athletes chose not to play all-white teams; and trade unions, where my fight was focused, led members into organised solidarity actions such as boycotts.

There were simple deeds, just as there were difficult ones, that gave citizens of all races the option to express their support for the resistance movement. The demand for the isolation of the apartheid regime became a tsunami, thundering at the gates of the citadels of power in the West.

It was hard enough, however, to achieve such a feat in a single country. To some, it might seem almost impossible to design a global campaign against injustice in a world with so many kinds of people, ideas and conflicts. Ideological shades of grey abound.

The difficulty lies in figuring out how to unite people despite their differences; to take divergent ideas, impassioned feelings and biases and turn them into actual tools which can be used for change. As a rookie labour organiser in South Africa in the seventies and eighties, I encountered much anger. I was angry myself. But my mentors in the union, as well as activist leaders such as Biko, persuaded me to use this energy in more constructive ways. My rage was pointless, unhealthy even, unless I utilised it to help build lasting productive movements that would eventually evolve into unstoppable forces of change. We encouraged this same kind of constructiveness in our members, who came to realise that the struggle for their rights in the factory was inextricably linked to the larger struggle for freedom. In both cases it was essential they came together as a united force to instil fear in those who suppressed them.

The Western world viewed us as a small group of terrorists, but after a few years and a lot of work we simply laughed off such antagonism. Our record books had the signatures of a million workers, all of whom had voluntarily become COSATU members and were willing to pay weekly subscriptions. They were all proud to call themselves supporters of an organisation for change.

It ultimately did not matter to us that a small group of people in South Africa denied our cause or questioned our reasons for being angry.

We were the *majority*. We had the mandate of the people.

This was the thing we kept in mind when we organised our movement. It should be the primary goal of every activist organisation as its leaders ask themselves constantly: *Are the people marching alongside us because it is in their best interests? Did we reach consensus about our objectives? Did we listen? Did we talk? Did we agree? Do we have a mandate? Did we find a way to go forward?*

If you can answer yes to all of these questions, then you are on the right path. If not – well, maybe it is time to start rethinking the mission. None of these terms are subjective. Their consequences are real enough to affect the lives of many people. The most difficult part about being a leader is having the courage to be honest with yourself and to walk against the populist tide when necessary. You need to know when to lead from the front, from the middle, and when to step back.

These were the hard lessons that carried me forward as I transitioned from being a student activist to a labour organiser. Now I am passing them on, humbly, to the next generation of activists.

7

Building Solidarity

D URING THE COLD WAR powerful economic and political elites in the West conspired to destroy the global union movement which they viewed as a manifestation of the 'red threat of communism'. There are still large influential workers' movements all over the world, but big business and government usually try to choke them into submission.

The defeat of Soviet-style communism and the rise of capitalism made unions vulnerable to the mercy of a unipolar world. Those were big victories for conservatives, who relished the opportunity to test out their pet theory of neoliberalism. Their aim? To exploit every aspect of society – governments, public institutions and entire populations – in order to generate more capital than such a small group of individuals would ever need. If the earth is devastated because of their actions, so be it. There would be so much money sloshing around that they could easily retreat to their lives of luxury, sheltered from all consequences, while the rest of the world dealt with the fallout.

In this new economic system the geographical locus of old-style industrial production and labour shifted to India and China. The global capitalist system now had over two billion people integrated into its industrial complex. China became the world's new factory, engaged in mostly low-skill production, while India heightened the range somewhat, including highly skilled services such as information technology and engineering in its industrial design.

The net effect was the reduction of wage levels in these developing countries, which impacted on unionisation and bargaining mechanisms. India, although ostensibly democratic, still operates under a social system that is autocratic and caste-based, and labour in China is subjected to the authoritarian oversight of its communist government. Western powers not only liberalised financial capital and outsourced production, but they helped the rise of poorly regulated and generally union-free environments which freely exploit their workers with long hours, bad wages and terrible working conditions.

In the 1990s, Bretton Woods institutions obtained a renewed mandate to drive structural adjustment policies and neoliberal agendas in the developing world.[1] This was known as the Washington Consensus, which promoted a narrative of 'one size fits all' through free trade, free markets, floating exchange rates and macroeconomic stability. Privatise, Deregulate and Liberalise were tattooed on the foreheads of the new Masters of the Universe, and Profit named the victor over the People. This new world economic policy allowed for fanatical market fundamentalism, which is driven by three institutions – the International Monetary Fund, the World Bank and the World Trade Organization – while the US dollar was given the most dominant position in the global economy. The US government could print as much money as it wanted without devaluing its currency and could run any trade deficit it wanted.

By the 1990s information capitalism formed the basis of global economic relations, obtaining its dominance from network technology, the mobile communications revolution and the emergence of the global marketplace. The state retreated and the market ruled, with banking executives and hedge fund managers becoming its high priests. The old model banking system, which consisted of mostly small family or co-op banks running a regulated system of low-risk, low-margin investment, was taken over by bigger institutions that loosened regulatory controls. Finance capital and large returns formed the heart of this metamorphosed structure.

On the surface, the major innovation of this system was the financialisation of assets based on derivatives which allowed banks to skim their profits off customers, clients and governments. In reality, however, it was a poisonous pyramid scheme, driven by a banking class powered by the 'too big to fail' ideology. So many layers of toxic debt were built onto this pyramid that it led to the global financial crisis of 2008, the worst financial crisis since the Great Depression.

Now was our moment as activists. A system that had generated a worldwide recession, further entrenched the global gulf of income inequality, caused wars over resources that initiated some of the greatest humanitarian crises in our history, and pushed us ever closer to an ecological precipice was now on its knees.

So did the activist community do anything to forge a bold and courageous alternative to neoliberal capitalism in the wake of its collapse?

To give the simple answer: no, we did not.

Civil society was fragmented, depoliticised and weakened by its dependency on donor aid from philanthropic organisations that had driven it into silo-based activities. Often its accountability was to bean counters that were only interested in validating their financial log frames rather than building the people-to-people solidarity that brings fundamental and lasting change. Civil society has become part of the problem. Our actions do not address the mounting anger and demand for systemic political and economic transformation demanded by our people.

The most forceful responses to the crisis originated in campaigns instigated by mostly young people in the West. Beginning in May 2011 with the Indignados movement in Spain, which spearheaded the country's anti-austerity protests, the fight against institutionalisation and socio-economic inequality blew up four months later with the Occupy Wall Street movement in New York. It was clear that the Arab resistance had sparked something in these Western protestors, a sense of communion with people who led lives and lived in worlds vastly different from their own. Many of the demonstrators who crowded Zuccotti Park in the Wall Street district were experiencing financial hardships similar to their Arab and Spanish counterparts – saddled with student debt or unable to find decent jobs.

The Occupy movement as a rally cry against the power of transnationals carries important lessons for those organising in the twenty-first century. Despite being a leaderless movement, it created a social resistance strategy that was built on organic movement from below. In the process, Occupy Wall Street helped bring the global inequality gap to the forefront of political news, capturing the imagination of the public with its slogan 'We are the 99%'. There were no elites participating in this campaign. It was not about individual struggle. By denying the media a charming outspoken leader capable of articulating a thirty-second sound bite, the Occupy movement placed an emphasis on the struggles of a global community – despite taking place in one of the wealthiest cities in the world. It reminded me of my experiences in the union movement, when workers of all cultures and backgrounds came together outside factories to call out as one 'Siyalala', or 'We are occupying'.

While these Western movements were issue-based and temporary, they can be seen in the same light as other leaderless mass protests which have since occurred, such as the Fallist campaign in South Africa and the Podemas in Spain, all of which encourage the youth to educate themselves in campaign organisation and to become active in local politics. They drew the battle lines of the new struggle against inequality which is capturing democracy across the world.

But the war is far from over, as illustrated in governments' continuous failure to put citizens' needs first. Firmly committed to policies protecting the increasingly narrow global plutocracy, the American government poured in close to $13 trillion to rescue its flailing banking system. Shamelessly, this colossal mountain of debt used taxpayers' money while imposing an austerity programme that slashed public services and social wages. The citizens, who had nothing to do with causing the crisis, ended up paying for it as their living standards diminished considerably.

The high-finance mafia that had started all the trouble in the first place walked away scot-free. Naturally, they returned to their old ways of doing business, concentrating more wealth into the hands of the 1 per cent.

Almost a decade after the crisis, no progress seems to have been made. The perpetrators of injustice remain at large, still rich and still powerful. Proof once again that the system will only serve those it believes have something to give it in return.

In my days as a casual worker in a textile factory, I witnessed just how far hierarchical authoritarian controls will go to squeeze out as much surplus value from their workers as they can.

In COSATU our strategy was pretty straightforward. Organise the working class, build our power at the point of production, and after we have seized political power at either the ballot box or in the streets, all we had to do was socialise the means of production.

A lot has changed since then. In fact, I would say nearly everything has changed. A technological revolution has fundamentally transformed our world and the way we live, work, play, access services and information, and communicate. It has altered the nature of work and production, wealth creation and economic growth, even in developing countries. In Africa, mobile phone penetration is now 67 per cent, enjoyed by 1.13 billion of the population, while the number of people connected to the internet is steadily increasing, estimated at 26.5 per cent in 2015.[2] More people than ever have the world's information at their fingertips, and yet Africa is still addicted to age-old ideologies and our non-virtual reality is dominated by institutions that are largely obsolete.

The shop floor is one area that has been greatly altered by mechanics and the technology boom. There are close to three billion labour jobs of some form or another around the world – nearly half of the world's population – even while work has become increasingly casual and outsourced, and the social wage has been reduced.[3] In a networked economy robotics, machines and artificial intelligence have become the moving force of mass production and labourers no longer make up the primary means of surplus value. Nearly half of the world's workers – approximately 40 per cent – are informal, creating a new power gap between labour and the top brass.[4]

The new challenge now is transforming the collective bargaining model that once was the lifeblood of the union movement and which has been undercut by informal remote work and an increase in service sector jobs.

In 2010, while attending a twenty-fifth anniversary celebration for COSATU, I realised just how out of touch the modern union movement is with current developments in information technology and social interaction. I could sense the awe of the young activists and campaigners I met there as we discussed the two million-strong labour movement. But they also shared their concerns about the direction in which it was heading in the post-apartheid era, when so many developments have made it impossible to approach union politics in the old conventional way. 'Comrade, the language is so old,' one activist said to me about the socialist thinking that still dominates union philosophy in the country. 'We cannot connect to these concepts and there are not many young people here.'

He captured perfectly the dilemma facing unions today, many of which have become increasingly out of touch with their members, considered mere extensions of the political elites. With the next generation of workers leaving a failing education system with few skills, there are even fewer prospects for formal jobs for our youth. Millions of highly skilled graduates in the developed world, saddled with debt, are already struggling to find work, and many have to take casual or low-paid jobs in the services or hospitality industries, or as taxi drivers.

The future of work as we know it is therefore vastly different from anything South Africans might have predicted at the end of 1994, when we were still running high on our new democracy. We now have to search for value to offer to a 'futureless' youth enraged at the inequalities, big and small, that they experience every day.

During the liberation struggle, our agenda was human dignity, the belief that all people have the fundamental human right to a fair wage, job security, protection against unfair dismissals, maternity rights and pensions. You know, all the stuff that allows people to feel like they are worthwhile members of civilisation.

Our primary focus was on the shop floor, but we also understood that our movement could not stop there, that we had to travel further, to the gates of parliament. We knew we could not deliver dignity without delivering political change first, because the country's political system was ultimately the main source of every social problem in South Africa. To end the oppression our workers lived under, we had to end apartheid first.

The establishment of COSATU was a major breakthrough for organised workers. As the struggle intensified in the 1980s and protests raged across the country, the apartheid government became more aggressive in its efforts to end rebellion, declaring numerous states of emergency. This made organising in the unions very hard.

The 1979 amendment of the Industrial Conciliation Act gave African unions further cause to come together to oppose the continued exploitation by the state of migrant workers. Through the amendment, the rights of African workers who lived in urban areas were given limited recognition by the government. Migrant workers, however, who made up the majority of the African labour force, were excluded from this new law.

This was a blatant attempt by the apartheid state to sow divisions in the African working class. In order to subvert their efforts and to strengthen the union cause, thirty-three unions, including FOSATU, decided to merge into one federation of unions. The entire process was extremely complex, requiring a fusing of our various political aims and philosophies so that we could present a unified front. After four long years of painstaking negotiations, and many stops and starts, the majority of the unions finally came together as COSATU on 1 December 1985.

The success of our new movement demanded a lot of work if COSATU was to be a dominant force for change. To increase our own influence, we had to continue curbing the authoritative influence of management in the workplace and to grow the power of working men and women – the final goal of all workers' unions.

Workers have leverage. Their sweat is essential to production. It is the job of the unions to build workers' power so that the profits accrued in the industry are shared fairly with those who do most of the work.

Credible negotiations can only be carried out by strong grass-roots organisations with a mandate from their constituents. COSATU's shop stewards knew they had to ensure speedy and accurate report-backs to workers, and obtain their approval before making any agreement. The first negotiation was always with membership, who would establish the set of demands. In every negotiation – worker rights and responsibilities as laid out in the union constitution, the details of settlements, disciplinary or grievance processes, and wage bargaining – the principle of democratic worker participation remained at the heart of each procedure.

Full-time officials who could not abide by this process, which was often painstaking and lengthy, did not last long in the union. Neither did shop stewards aspiring to be managers, who were summarily replaced. There were also severe consequences if leaders or officials met management alone or misused union funds.

Worker–union relations were not one-sided, however. Our members understood that negotiations were about give and take. Every so often a compromise was required, but this was only with their full agreement. Many times, especially during strikes and mass dismissals, loss of jobs meant being shipped out to a Bantustan or neighbouring country and placed on a permanent blacklist. Our supporters understood the importance of being part of a union and working with it to ensure it maintained its negotiating power with management.

As in most successful unions, there were no victors or vanquished in COSATU. Workers did not want to burn the factory down. They wanted meaningful progress and they wanted to participate in that change. Above all, they wanted to be recognised as equal human beings with their own rights and privileges.

A focus on shared interests was our permanent goal, regardless of the context.

The newly formed Congress of South African Trade Unions made an early decision not to use the union as a conveyor belt into politics. Instead, we formed alliances. The Mass Democratic Movement, established in 1988 as a loose coalition of COSATU and the United Democratic Front, was an umbrella body consisting of thousands of grassroots movements and non-governmental organisations (NGOs), and was another attempt at resisting extreme apartheid repression at that time. We also chose to align with the ANC, led by the likes of Nelson Mandela, Oliver Tambo and Chris Hani, as the party had a tried-and-tested track record, a history of strategic and militant mass struggle, and a philosophy that recognised the significance of having an organised working class on its side. And while the MDM would end up representing a massive flotilla of organisations, the core was always COSATU and mass social movements of women, youth and other sectors of civil society.

As an activist, I had very strong ideological views, but I learnt the hard way not to shove my politics down the throats of members.

When I did, we ended up with huge divisions, such as those between COSATU's leadership and a conservative tribal-based movement called the Inkatha Freedom Party (IFP). In my role as a union organiser in Pietermaritzburg in 1980, and coming from the Black Consciousness Movement, I expressed harsh views of Inkatha and its divisive tribalist culture, arrogantly proclaiming that no right-thinking worker leader would support a cultural movement that held power in a self-governing Bantustan. In student politics, such disputes and debates were the norm. But on the factory floor, these kinds of assumptions seemed naive and were ultimately wrong. The majority of workers, it turns out, felt their political home was Inkatha.

Along with union leaders, I decided to stick to the mandate that had made unionism successful, and which led to COSATU becoming such a dominant force in the labour movement. *To build a successful organisation, we had to concentrate on creating a shared vision around the bread-and-butter interests of our people.* The intellectual arrogance of middle-class activists often creates the biggest obstacles to healthy, constructive discourse in political groups. Activists need to know how to work within and outside a variety of power systems, including those of traditional or religious organisations. So as COSATU's rivalry with the IFP became more heated, I realised it would be suicidal for us to take on any more battles, ideological or otherwise, that we could not win.

Politics is not just about militant slogans, radical demands and blustering speeches. It is not just about knowing what you are against, but also knowing what you are for. Following the launch of COSATU, we made the mistake of taking on too many conflicts at once – against the apartheid state, white capital, Inkatha and the old sweetheart unions who took their orders from white bosses. We did this as a fragile federation of thirty-three unions that was still trying to formulate a common narrative between our numerous factions, and without a bank account, offices or staff.

In May 1986, five months after the establishment of COSATU, the IFP started its own trade union, the United Workers' Union of South Africa (UWUSA), with the intention of becoming the leading union for the country's black labourers, even though it was partially sponsored by the apartheid police. At their inauguration, which took place in a packed stadium with over 60 000 supporters, members of the new union carried a coffin bearing my name and that of our president, Elijah Barayi, in a symbolic gesture of UWUSA's aim to bury COSATU.

UWUSA members in the labour force then initiated a violent war with their COSATU co-workers, determined to break what they believed to be an external functionary of the ANC and all forms of militant unionism, which was a prerogative of management as well. Factory by factory, our members had to fight to defend themselves, some even dying during the confrontations. Hundreds of clashes took place when UWUSA launched attacks against COSATU, the first starting at a coal mine near Vryheid in June 1986, when eleven members of COSATU were killed and 115 others injured.

It is not surprising that most of the labourers in the South African workforce ended up choosing COSATU as the union to represent their interests. It was imperative for us that we always showed our members how important they were to our organisation. The union belonged to the workers, not to authoritarian leaders looking to serve their own agendas and engage in violent battles. Tens of thousands of workers democratically elected our leadership every year, and what they wanted was the central focus of every major discussion in the union and with management.

Every meeting was like a workshop, as all our leaders came together to learn about other cultures, and to read and write and study. We understood that educating our leaders on a variety of subjects would furnish them with the right skills to make better negotiations and to recruit more members.

The shift in political allegiance towards COSATU was therefore a conscious and deliberate decision by the workers. It was not imposed from above or decided during discussions in workshops. *COSATU won its battle because we were rooted in the workplace and built alliances with communities who trusted us. The union was the workers' university. Political education is a process, not an event.*

We did not achieve this by transforming the union into a fashionable activist school that spent all its time discussing political theory. We had to *co-create the vision* of what we wanted, not just within union management, but, more importantly, with our members. It was about building political theory alongside the democratic practice and with careful, steady planning. *I learnt that timing was everything.*

As change came closer in the mid-eighties and political liberation seemed within our grasp, we decided that we would have to pursue a more comprehensive programme of restructuring the country's economic and industrial landscape to ensure the centrality of working people in the new state.

It was our job to constantly reflect on our members' futures and to fight for progress both in material and political terms, on the factory floor and in society. We had to remain on the outside of our struggle as well, making the outside the inside.

How many activists do that today?

As more civil institutions and labour movements become bogged down by their political commitments, the needs of their constituents are pushed to the wayside. Often they get tied to a rhetoric of regime change and lose their independence, becoming mere adjuncts of larger, more powerful parties. This has an obvious and major drawback for supporters, because if the union or political party of your choice loses power, you lose power. You are just voting fodder for the next election.

To me, the decision for a labour movement to transform into a political party or to go into government is absurd.

Labour movements have produced great political leaders, and

will continue to. But the moment a leader leaves the fold, they become just another player at the table. It might be tempting for unions to view their constituencies as a power base for moving their organisations in another direction, but it is integral that they remain independent of all of their political affiliations. Unions exist to work on behalf of their supporters, not to use their supporters to fulfil their leaders' ambitions.

Being part of the formation of COSATU was the most profound organisational experience of my life. It taught me so much about people – how to organise and negotiate with them, and how to find common ground in an often violent and adversarial climate.

Change, be it political, social or otherwise, encompasses the art of coalition building.

When broad coalitions work they are organised around a simple message and specific goal that can transform the lives of millions of people. Look at the years-long campaign to convince people travelling in vehicles to wear their seatbelts. While many viewed this as government interference in their private affairs, partnerships between groups in both the public and private sectors eventually succeeded in persuading millions that it was the safest thing to do while driving. Today, thanks to wide-ranging advocacy and count-less awareness campaigns, it has become second nature for most people to put on their seatbelts the moment they get into a car. Countless lives have been saved as a result, including my own son's.

All organisations should regard building and maintaining coali-tions as an integral part of their philosophy. Unions, which represent a large number of people of various backgrounds and personalities, are fertile terrain for conflict. Everything from petty office politics to fiery political debates form the basis of everyday union interac-tions. These disputes should be approached diplomatically, albeit in different ways and with appropriate levels of input.

In the 1980s COSATU crafted many coalitions, some strategic, others temporary. At the time many seemed unlikely or impossible, such as our alliances with faith-based movements and businesses. Our chief antagonists were not only white supremacists but powerful black conservative and traditional organisations such as the IFP. We had to train hard enough so we could dribble the ball through the goalposts of compromise and unity, doing so by sticking to our core issues and making the coalition sizeable enough that multiple interests were served. Above all, we never ever forgot about our members.

This is not how movements are organised in South Africa today. Violence seems to be ingrained in our culture, considered a legitimate means of expressing our grievances, even if the innocent or defenceless suffer the consequences. Consider the actions of protesting residents in the town of Vuwani in Limpopo, who burnt down twenty-four schools in mid-2016 to protest against the demarcation lines of a new municipality in the area. Most hurt by their actions are the children in their community, who require an education if they are ever to escape the dire circumstances into which they have been born. The motivation behind these acts seems unfathomable on the face of it.

But for many South Africans frustrated by the unchecked corruption of our government and widespread poverty and inequality, violence is often seen as the only way to communicate with our leaders; the only language they will understand. As violence is usually met with more violence, however, demonstrators who employ it become locked in a cycle of hostility. Protests by many activists are reduced to press statements, faceless crowds marching on the streets and filling stadiums while echoing the populist rhetoric of their leaders. No systematic attempt is made to organise street by street, village by village, and the outcome of this is a change of guard, not change in the lives of our people.

Through my experiences as a union organiser, I learnt that activism requires you to take calculated, often dangerous risks to obtain your objectives. My abiding lesson is that what activists *do* lasts longer in the memory of the people than what they *say*.

Be absolutely honest about potential threats to the people you work with and the communities you are organising. Confronting a brutal enemy can get people hurt or killed. An organisation that took many years to build can be obliterated in one day, while communities or factories suffering a major loss may take years to recover.

In COSATU we gained our victories by constantly increasing our bargaining chips with management over issues such as competitive wages and leave, trying to curtail their arbitrary power over workers. We did not see burning down a factory as a viable means of persuading our opponents to listen to us. This would have fuelled the conflict and lost our members jobs. There is a difference between maximum and minimum demands, as well as appropriate methods of giving voice to them. The petitions we made were backed up by data, such as the cost of living and daily needs of our members and their families.

We knew that every negotiation involves compromise. Negotiating is an art demanding skill, persuasion and influence. At the end of the day, each side has to return to its constituents and sell a deal. A winner-takes-all scenario never works, and it is essential that leaders establish a level of trust between negotiating teams. The same principles apply to political negotiations.

When Mandela described F.W. de Klerk, the last president under apartheid, as a 'man of integrity', that did not give the white government authority to impose unreasonable demands during talks preceding democracy. Instead, Mandela was showing his willingness to search for common ground on which to stand with another leader with whom he was engaging.

The strategic goal of any negotiation is therefore to navigate the minefield of vested interests and to build an agenda of shared interests. That is why South Africa is still regarded as a political phenomenon, a democracy that somehow, seemingly by a miracle, rose out of a negotiated revolution.

The impact of compromise and cooperation cannot be under-estimated.

This is also why one of COSATU's main aims was to break down the cultural barriers between workers that management had been nurturing for years to keep them divided. Apartheid may have been built on the back of a migrant labour system that separated black South Africans from one another, but as far as COSATU was concerned, hostels for Zulus, hostels for Shangaans and hostels for Xhosas were to be no more. Our members had to work together if we expected to convince management of our immense power as a unified organisation.

Our unity was the foundation of our strength and ultimately the backbone of our new democracy.

We must be wary of once again relying on such divisions to build narrow constituencies based on tribalism, ethnicity, patriarchy, language or religion. Zero tolerance should be shown for such attitudes. The only kind of movement that can protect against tribalism, nationalism and xenophobia is a social one that espouses non-racialism.

COSATU never centralised its leadership by installing a 'big chief' at the head of the organisation. Like a hydra, a mythological water serpent with numerous heads, there was more than one mind guiding our movement.

If we relied on individuals, the union would be destroyed. Top leaders were easy to take down, and as soon as they were picked off, management would exploit such divisions. That is why we needed real power on the factory floor. In such a structure, even if all of COSATU's leaders were weakened or unable to perform our duties, the government would never be able to wipe out what we had already created. There were too many of us. In 1987, when apartheid security forces bombed our headquarters, our cause did not lose a single day.

The only thing that can bring any institution to its knees is barren leadership. But it is difficult for leaders to be inept or corrupt if they follow organisational procedures. Then the movement itself functions as leader. COSATU's shop stewards, the men and women forming the essence of our union, were also its leaders. Eventually there were just too many of us to take down.

Leaders had to be disciplined in following union rules if they wanted our movement to be successful. They had to show initiative and drive, too, in order to communicate effectively with their comrades. These are permanent, inflexible principles, as were our commitments to democracy, unity, non-racialism and non-sexism. All other commitments are tactics, changed according to circumstance.

This is how we built a successful movement. What we did can still work today, but it will entail discipline and effort, not violence and rash behaviour.

So let us constantly reflect on how we did it in the past.

8

Managing Transition

IN 1990 THE apartheid regime was nearing its end. It had not been defeated militarily, but apartheid leaders knew the end of white rule was near. For many who fought in the liberation struggle, it was a surprise how quickly it came.

After decades of mass struggle it was the intensity of the 1989 Campaign of Defiance against Unjust Laws that ultimately broke the camel's back. During this time millions of black South Africans actively defied the racist laws and prohibitions preventing us from participating in everyday society. We showed up at white hospitals demanding treatment, occupied parks and beaches that were reserved for whites, and organised public meetings of groups that had been banned. In numerous public protests around the country we faced the police head on as they tried to keep us behind their barricades. None of us were willing to tolerate any longer the rules that took our citizenship away from us.

This was the critical moment when a regime loses its legitimacy and the people lose their fear. The burning embers of anger and discontent had become a raging bushfire of revolution.

Soon afterwards, on 2 February 1990, F.W. de Klerk announced that Nelson Mandela would be released from prison the following week and that all political organisations, including the ANC, were unbanned. Tata Madiba, the symbol of our resistance, was free. South Africa was on the road to a new future.

But many of us who were organisers in the struggle still had concerns.

Most revolutions fail because too little attention is paid to managing the transition from the old system to the new system. Those of us operating in South Africa's evolved political landscape therefore asked ourselves constantly what the future of our country should look like. We needed to achieve a post-apartheid dream of freedom not only in name, but in reality too. We had to figure out the length of time it would take to complete the transition and determine how we would govern such a completely transformed country.

We began by planning for this transition even before it arrived, determined to destroy, and never to utilise, the brutality and exclusion that had been the weapons of our oppressors. Our own stock of weaponry contained the values and objectives that we upheld during the decades of mass struggle preceding democracy, and we focused on preparing and unifying as many of our people as possible for this event.

There were many challenges confronting us. Powerful individuals who had played major roles in carrying out apartheid repression remained in control of the army and security forces. The beginning of the nineties was marked by violent conflicts between the ANC and black conservative forces such as Inkatha who were in alliance with white extremists. Hundreds of people died during these battles, and it looked like the country was teetering on the brink of a full-scale civil war.

As leaders of the resistance movement we knew we had little time to create a peaceful transition to democracy. We had to build a consensus with our main negotiating party, the National Party, and prevent them from using their veto in government to maintain the white minority's racial privileges. The right-wing threat of a counter-revolution also had to be neutralised if we were to prevail in implementing democracy.

The birth of freedom in South Africa, as anywhere else in the world, was fraught with strife. There were, and still are, cliques in every corner resistant to change and prepared to employ violent methods to achieve their ends. But the key objective of the anti-apartheid movement was a negotiated revolution. We had to develop an institutional framework that would promote peace and assist us in co-governing various elements of the transition, especially the activities of the security forces and the conduct of political parties operating at local level. The process required rules about how to interact with these factions so we could manage our differences and begin to formulate a common narrative that included all South Africans.

In the labour movement we drew from our knowledge of conflict resolution to try to reduce discord in communities. We approached business leaders with whom we had negotiated in the past to settle major strikes and labour disputes, and asked church leaders to help us mediate conflicts between rival COSATU and IFP supporters in the workplace. Our objective was to create an honest peaceful environment that guaranteed freedom of speech, association and assembly.

Nelson Mandela was a paradigm of a powerful negotiating force during this period. His defining genius was always his affinity for searching for solutions to some of the most complex challenges we faced in the country. In the negotiating period before democracy, the key issues were avoiding war, securing peace between opposing factions and creating the groundwork for a negotiated political revolution. Using the vast stores of empathy and tolerance at his disposal, Mandela was able to break through the walls of fear and hatred that our white compatriots hid behind and to establish a commonality with them, a shared interest in democracy.

At the same time, Mandela had the wisdom to recognise those moments when he should not give way.

This is always a challenge in times of fundamental change. Powerful individuals within our own ranks argued that we needed to counter violence with violence in order to defend ourselves. Mandela resisted this approach throughout the negotiating process. He called for a unilateral ceasefire after the Boipatong massacre on 17 June 1992, when forty-five residents in the Boipatong township were killed by IFP-affiliated steelworkers from a nearby hostel. By doing this, *Mandela resisted the urge to be demagogic and instead rose above the fray, swimming against the tide of popular sentiment and arguing for peace. This is real leadership.*

Militarism can sometimes be a problem in resistance struggles. Many freedom fighters are firm believers in that old military adage 'in order to save the village, we had to destroy it'. Blow up the bridges, bomb the radio stations, raze the farms, destroy the schools. And once the enemy is driven out, the soldiers march into what is left of the town and declare their victory. Whatever had been built by the people over decades or centuries is destroyed in almost an instant by their so-called liberators. It is always much easier to invade than it is to occupy.

In the mid-eighties we fiercely debated the necessity of establishing 'liberated' zones in KwaZulu-Natal that sought to obstruct or inhibit any violence from Inkatha and the state. Young activists angrily drove anyone suspected of being an Inkatha sympathiser or member out of townships where a majority of people supported the MDM. But this opened up these townships to massive and sustained attacks from regiments of fully armed IFP combatants supported by the security forces. Hundreds of people ended up dying during these skirmishes. The state is always better armed than its people and will not hesitate to use force against those who challenge its authority.

In these unpredictable and violent contexts, the language of war replaces the consolidating power of mass organisation by the people. I have seen the consequences of this kind of approach in failed states around the world. I have heard thousands of horror stories that should never form part of the narrative of our own country's fate.

There are never simplistic solutions in situations that involve many divergent interests. One-size-fits-all answers are rare, but past struggles do contain significant lessons for future groups of organisers. Negotiation and compromise help to build trust and offer a number of paths towards the fulfilment of a joint objective. It is essential, however, that activists understand that every context provides new challenges or conditions. Ideas and programmes should therefore be adapted so that they can function within these changed environments.

When we were preparing for South Africa's transition, the leadership of the resistance understood this. We carried out our responsibilities with integrity, a clear purpose and a deep organic connection to our mass base. Our dream was for a country united around the idea of one person, one vote, in a united, non-racial, non-sexist and democratic South Africa.

Undoubtedly we achieved that. But that was just one building block in the completion of the revolution yielding the fruits of freedom. There were others that were required to transform our economy and deracialise land ownership in the country.

On 14 September 1991, after a marathon series of talks, twenty-seven political organisations signed the National Peace Accord (NPA), which aimed to put an end to political violence in South Africa and create conditions for a peaceful political transition. A National Peace Secretariat was established to settle political conflicts across the country through local peace committees, and an estimated 15 000 peace monitors were trained in conflict resolution to help facilitate a smooth transition process. This was a campaign for peace that inspired ordinary citizens to participate in the creation of democracy, and worked at opposing the extremist factions in political parties that were inciting violence.

We started building a consensus on political tolerance and resolving conflict through dialogue, street by street, factory by factory, and township by township.

The police were also held to account for any involvement in initiating conflict. Every police vehicle contained a log book and could be identified by a large painted number on its side. This made it easier for victims of police violence to back up their claims. And it was a warning to rogue elements in the police force that there were serious consequences for those who stirred up conflict.

In my capacity as general secretary of COSATU, I attended numerous meetings, mostly at police stations, where I negotiated the conditions of mass marches, voter-education drives and rallies. My fellow arbiters were police commanders, representatives of warring parties, as well as church and business leaders.

But it is safe to say that the instrument which afforded us the clearest path towards a negotiated settlement was the National Peace Accord. It not only helped to rein in security forces and bring them under civilian control, but, along with Mandela's effective wooing of the right-wing to join the democratic process, the NPA neutralised those powerful destabilising forces that were preventing a peaceful move away from apartheid. Most importantly, the accord acted as a forerunner to the formal talks of the Convention for a Democratic South Africa, or CODESA, as well as to the formation of a Transitional Executive Committee.

The CODESA process was hardly a smooth one. At its first congress, which took place on 20 December 1991, nineteen organisations were present, including the ANC, the National Party, the SACP and the IFP. The convention – at which so many groups were providing their input on a variety of issues – naturally became a battleground for debate and dispute.

Our transition was never going to be easy. It required us to follow a sequence of significant steps before eventually reaching a shared vision for a new country. Even the creation of South Africa's constitution followed a lengthy process and was only finalised by parliament in 1996, two years after the first democratic elections.

Irrespective of the disputes that arose during the CODESA process, or the criticisms laid at its door for not fully anticipating the challenges South Africa faces today, it still played a crucial role in the settlement for a non-racial, democratic state. The value of the contribution that CODESA made to the struggle continues to be debated by historians and the current generation of activists. Some consider its inability to formulate fundamental policies for restructuring the economy and land distribution as a betrayal of South Africans looking forward to living in a more equal society. This is a legitimate argument, although it overlooks what I believe to have been the primary goal of the CODESA process, which was to negotiate a peaceful political solution for every individual and group that would have to live and coexist in the new South Africa.

In this respect, it accomplished its mandate. That was the political project of Mandela's generation. Everything else that has been done to undermine our freedom happened on our watch, the generation that followed the inspiring founding father of our democracy.

While unique to South Africa in many ways, CODESA and its achievements can more fully be appreciated by considering the period in which it occurred, when many other transitions, successful or otherwise, were taking place in countries around the world. Compare conditions in South Africa today with those of the ex-Soviet republics such as Ukraine; Germany following the fall of the Berlin Wall; and countries that became independent in the nineties, such as Bosnia, Chile and Eritrea. Like South Africa, these nations were designing their future, trying to forge agreements that would encompass and protect the largest number of people. Many were unable to succeed in this new climate of governance and have become states that are a strange hybrid of oligarchic rule and quasi-democracy.

In many respects, South Africa's transition from a formerly

oppressive racist regime into a successful democracy was an exceptional and even unique event. As the country moved towards its first democratic elections in 1994, it seemed as if justice had finally been won for those who were excluded and displaced under apartheid. We were close to real transformative political power and now had to use it to protect what we had built from corruption and greed – the two forces that have brought down so many newly independent and democratic states. Those of us who fought in the struggle, who knew what sacrifices were demanded for genuine political change, told ourselves that South Africans would never again experience the degradation of segregation and servitude to an oppressive government.

We actually believed this.

But therein lie the lessons of history.

9

The Challenge
of Democracy

HISTORY IS ALWAYS contested. Monuments are built and then toppled. The names of streets, towns and airports are changed. Books are written or rewritten. Memories fade.

For those of us who were born under apartheid, the end of its repressive rule was met with profound joy and relief. And while we would never forget the indignities and wrongs of the past, we were also determined to create a new future for our citizens free from resentment and pain.

There was an atmosphere of deliverance surrounding the first democratic elections of 27 April 1994, when I, along with millions of others, cast my first vote as a South African citizen. It was a right for which many had been prepared to die, and as we wept, laughed and sang, it seemed almost unreal that the moment had finally arrived.

'Never, never and never again shall it be that this beautiful land will again experience the oppression of one by another and suffer the indignity of being the skunk of the world ... Let freedom reign,' Madiba proclaimed during his inauguration speech on 10 May 1994, when he was declared South Africa's first black president.

Suddenly, after decades of struggle, black South Africans were in power. As one of 400 newly inaugurated members of parliament (MPs), I was part of a system of government that had the authority to utilise this power for good.

The Government of National Unity (GNU) functioned under the mandate of an interim constitution and was led by the ANC, which won a large majority of the votes in 1994. It was a hodgepodge of old political hands, battle-weary warriors, political neophytes, and community and union leaders. What we lacked was broad experience, and Mandela knew it. He also understood the extent of the challenges confronting us.

Although some structures, instituted during apartheid, were already in place, the country was still behind in many other developmental areas. For decades black South Africans had been neglected by the apartheid government, denied rights to the most basic of services. In 1994 our country needed everything. We had to build schools, clinics, hospitals, roads and electricity grids and open up the modern state to the majority of its citizens, many of whom lived in townships, slums and villages with little or no infrastructure.

COSATU, which had played a prominent role in community development and activism since its formation in 1985, was determined to be part of this reconstructive phase of South African history. This is why we decided to form an alliance with the ANC and the SACP in the run-up to the 1994 elections.

It is a decision about which I am asked quite often. The federation, which had a massive support base, could easily have sat out the negotiation process and left our members to vote as they saw fit. But COSATU was also the strongest mass-based organisation during this period, and we believed that forming an alliance with two other powerful organisations would help us formulate a programme that could bring a more peaceful transition into democracy. Once this was achieved, we would then use the alliance to fulfil specific goals of development that placed the needs of the majority before anything else.

There was an alternative, and that was to create a stand-alone labour party that would function as the sharp point of the country's left-wing spear. But this would have been a complicated matter because of our large web of partners. We also trusted the ANC and respected our members' overriding support of the party and its leadership. COSATU went for what we thought at the time to be a win-win situation, and we felt excited to be part of a gigantic movement with so much support, that represented so much of what we believed in, and that we thought was committed to effecting fundamental transformation. It turned out to be a decision that carried major consequences.

While my experience in parliament was certainly instructive, it was by no means the only option available to COSATU to influence government. Had I not become a member of parliament or a minister, South Africa would have had 399 other MPs to help run the state. If COSATU had chosen not to cross over into the alliance, there would still have been several other parties running the country. We made the decision we thought was best for our people at the time.

Of course hindsight, as they say, provides perfect vision. Perhaps it would have been better for COSATU to have remained an independent movement given how quickly the Tripartite Alliance turned into a conduit for foraging votes at election time. If we had chosen not to align with any political parties, we could have returned to fully pursuing our old prerogatives of strengthening mass social causes and remaining a check on the power of political elites and their apparatchiks.

We had always known that once a labour movement loses its independence, when it forms part of a structure that it should continually challenge, it becomes a mere cog in the political instrument and loses its purpose. And the goal of the ANC, like any political party, is to stay in power. I had many discussions with Chris Hani in which we discussed these issues. Even though he was one of the struggle's most passionate fighters and a leader in both MK and the SACP, he chose to stay out of government because he believed South Africa needed a mass movement that would turn its sights to defending the revolution. Days before his assassination on 10 April 1993, Hani offered his opinions on what South Africa's future rulers might look like in a setting which had transferred all political power to them: 'The perks of a new government are not really appealing to me. Everybody would like to have a good job, a good salary ... but for me that is not the be-all of the struggle.' He then voiced his greatest fear, which was that 'the liberators emerge as elitists ... who drive around in Mercedes-Benzes and use the resources of this country ... to live in palaces and to gather riches'.[1]

His prediction hit the nail on the head.

Parliamentary salaries were indeed generous, as were car and travel allowances. Never before had I had access to such wealth. I learnt very quickly that power is corrupting – or perhaps it is that power attracts the corrupt.

The greatest mistake South Africans made was to assume that a democratic government would by default have our best interests at heart. COSATU's joining of the alliance was indicative of its belief that our influence in government would effect genuine change, partly because we thought our political allies wanted the same thing. We had mobilised workers behind the Reconstruction and Development Programme (RDP), which sought to redress the economic and social legacy of apartheid and to restore land and resources to the people who had been denied these rights. For us, democracy was more than simply having the right to vote every five years, but a means of ensuring that every citizen in our country possessed the most basic human rights – homes, water, sanitation, electricity, quality healthcare and education. In the minds of COSATU's leaders, the RDP was the ideological glue that would hold us together as a nation because its roots were firmly planted in the premise of the 1955 Freedom Charter, which promised that the 'national wealth of our country, the heritage of all South Africans, shall be restored to the people'.

The RDP created a vision for the future of South Africa as a people-centred democracy that would empower shop stewards, community leaders and farmworkers to set the agenda for radical change in our country. The people would be the main players in negotiations for the economic transition, and public policy, not government policy, would drive our transformation.

But it did not occur to us that the ANC would not share our ideals. The RDP was barely in place for two years, and had been laying the groundwork for massive change in local communities, when divisions started emerging between members of the alliance. Much of the time before this had been spent consulting with communities, establishing a multi-stakeholder consensus, designing programmes that would fundamentally speed up development, and building political and economic structures that would have the capacity to implement our policies. The full scope of our plans never came to fruition, however. The political arrogance of the ANC's primary view of itself as the 'elected democratic leadership' conflicted with COSATU's notion of South Africa as a 'development state', and began to overtake all meaningful discussion in our ranks.

A new statist narrative emerged which made our people mere bystanders in the development process and pitted 'pragmatists and realists' on the one side against so-called utopian idealists on the other. In complete secrecy, a plot was devised by a cabal that operated outside traditional ANC structures, the Tripartite Alliance and even the cabinet and parliament in order to terminate the RDP initiative. The RDP office was closed within weeks and a new strategy known as GEAR (Growth, Employment and Redistribution) became the programme for advancing development in South Africa. In one Stalinist process, the entire social consensus between the alliance partners and the majority of citizens, which we had been building for decades, was destroyed.

It was an event that still informs the broken trust between citizens and government today. I felt that this was one of those rare occasions when Mandela acted like an orthodox president, responding to false fears about an amorphous market and giving in to the idea that we had to follow the rest of the world and adopt a neoliberal economic policy.

This was not something for which I had signed up. I had vowed to change the old system, not to be co-opted by it, and I was shocked that Mandela had given in to the technocrats in the party rather than choose what was best for his people. The entire situation left me disillusioned and I wanted to resign. But after discussing the issue with my trusted circle of family and friends, I decided to remain in government and accept the position of communications minister. It was clear to me by then that the political culture in the new South Africa was changing. The country's government appeared to be reverting to an old system of rule that would uphold an imperial presidency. With Mandela's announcement that he would only be in office for one term, I knew that my work in government would come to an end at the same time, in 1999.

My decision to become a member of parliament marked the end of another phase of my organisational life. Now I had a new end in my future. The journey was not without its rewards, however, as government work, which was very different from my duties in the union, offered me an insider's view of how ruling parties function and the decisions that determine their success or failure as representatives of the people.

Whether or not governments act on all of their constituents' needs or wants, the relationship between them does not have to be contentious or fraught. Government should always be regarded as a 'frenemy' rather than an outright nemesis, a partner who has to be challenged and disputed constantly if we are to get anything from it. It is *our* government after all. We, the people, put it into power. In the new government of democratic South Africa, many of its leaders were comrades who had fought against a rule of law that excluded millions from privileges to which they had a rightful share.

None of us wanted a parallel system in the new South Africa, but rather an effective government that served all of its citizens, irrespective of their political or ethnic shade.

Flash-forward two decades to the modern South African state in 2017 and the ANC well into its fifth term as ruling party. It is evident that the dreams we had at the onset of liberation were just that – the empty aspirations of a government that believed itself to be completely different from and morally superior to its apartheid predecessors. State capture is now our continued reality, and a government with a new face – that of the liberator – uses the country's institutions as vehicles for accumulating wealth and power.

It is not all as bad as it sometimes seems, however. We are still a robust democracy, and this has led to some noisy and messy affairs. There have been many victories, but also many mistakes. South Africa continues to face many challenges, including rampant corruption, institutionalised racism, a failing education system and the HIV/AIDS pandemic. But we have to keep confronting these problems head on, figuring out what parts of them are fixable and then determining solutions to lessen their destructive impact.

This may sound obvious, almost banal, but many South Africans who are angry about the current state of their country seem to have forgotten that a positive outcome was never an inevitability for our country.

Political parties pursue power, and when they obtain it, they endeavour to keep it. The rest of society – unions, civil groups, individuals, the press – have a permanent duty to keep government in check at all times and without fail. We have a number of mechanisms at our disposal to ensure government does its job, made available to us by our democratic institutions, rights and privileges. To speak out against laws or decisions we believe are violating our rights, we can engage in protests, write exposés, pursue our own investigations, file lawsuits and, of course, punish parties at the polls for poor performance.

In the 2016 municipal elections, the ANC's loss of the major metros Johannesburg, Tshwane (Pretoria) and Nelson Mandela Bay (Port Elizabeth) – in addition to Cape Town, which it had lost ten years earlier – was proof that many in its constituency, particularly those in urban areas, were no longer prepared to tolerate the party's corrupt and inept governance of their cities.

By not participating actively in moderating government power, it becomes easy for those in power to co-opt the checks and balances that exist to keep them in line. They become tools of the ruling party's machinery and democracy is essentially lost. Citizens can no longer participate when laws are changed or created, but have to follow the whims of autocrats who operate with deception and secrecy.

This is what happened to COSATU following the breakdown of the RDP initiative. The ANC's betrayal should have motivated the organisation to withdraw from the alliance and refocus its mission on the people who gave us our purpose – the workers. Instead, the union became a conveyer belt for the destructive policies and selfish aims of a political elite. We should have placed more pressure on the ANC to stand by its promises. With no barriers left to keep the party in line, it was free to capture the state's wealth and create a patronage network that exists only to enrich a small number of individuals.

In Africa today 80 per cent of the continent's wealth rests in the hands of 100 000 people. Three individuals control more wealth than 50 per cent of the South African population.[2]

This unfair and brutal system of governance can no longer be sustained. It is destroying societies, the environment, and the dignity that countless revolutions and resistance struggles have sought to gain for the oppressed.

It is time we initiate a struggle for a new future and inspire a revolution against our current oppressors.

The age-old question, of course, is how to begin.

10

Lessons of the Lula Moment

B RAZIL'S SOCIO-ECONOMIC and political situation is currently a mess. As a close ideological ally of South Africa, it acts
somewhat like a mirror to the political narrative unfolding in our
own country and the direction in which we as a newly democratic
developing country might be headed. In the first quarter of 2016,
Brazil's economy, the largest in Latin America, shrank by 5.4 per cent,
while unemployment rose by 11.2 per cent in the period between
April 2015 and February 2016. Just a few months before Brazil would
be hosting the Olympics in August of that year, it was facing its
largest recession since the 1930s.[1]

Getting to its current state has been a long process, but, as it is in
any country, getting out of it will also be a process. Although Brazil
faces many challenges at present, there is no reason to believe that
any of them are unbeatable, or that they invalidate the progress
made in its recent past. The election in 2003 of Brazil's first leftist
president, the iconic Luiz Inácio Lula da Silva, or 'Lula', was a ground-
breaking moment in the nation's history. As a former metal worker
and leader of Brazil's Workers' Party (PT), he was able to break
through some of the barriers of classism and racism in the country

– remnants of its colonial past – and inspire constructive interactions between its more than 200 million citizens. Lula was president from 2003 to 2010, and was succeeded by Dilma Rousseff, also from the PT. Rousseff was impeached in 2016 in what many believe was a constitutional coup and was succeeded by Michel Temer, from the rightist Brazilian Democratic Movement, who has been implicated in corruption scandals himself.

Brazil is a key player in the South–South alignment, which has seen developing nations from Africa, South America and Asia form joint agreements on trade, investment, resources and policy to increase their influence in global politics, currently dominated by wealthy countries in the West. The alignment is the developing world's attempt to help co-determine the way the world is governed, to take back control of their own valuable resources.

Whether Brazil will continue to play an effective role in the South–South Cooperation depends on how it chooses to sort out its economy and the corruption in its government. The last several years have certainly been instructive and are full of lessons for countries like South Africa, also struggling to deal with the destructive impact of corruption and the betrayal of a government that had once been a liberator.

In June 2012 I had the honour of meeting with Lula during one of his visits to South Africa. The former Brazilian president was sixty-six at the time and had just recovered from cancer. Nevertheless, he patiently answered all of the questions my nineteen-year-old son Kami had for him, displaying an immense capacity for listening and attentiveness – a quality that Mandela also possessed.

When I asked Lula what he considered to be his greatest achievement as president, he gave an answer surprising for a politician. 'The biggest legacy of my presidency is not the programmes that took thirty million Brazilians out of absolute poverty and created fifteen million jobs. It was the accountability of the public institutions and real partnership with business, labour and civil society that brought hope to the people. We put the needs of the people first. Not ours.'

Lula chooses not to focus on the statistics and numbers of his presidency, but rather on the social cohesion he helped create, which was built on trust and transparency – an openness that character-ised every government activity and institution from the ground up. 'I was not the president,' he said. 'The people were the president. The foundation of the "Brazilian Miracle" is not mine. It is that of the people. If I failed my people who elected me, it would be the people failing, and the poor would be proving their critics right that we did not have what it takes to rule,' Lula reiterated.

In Lula's first term he launched the Zero Hunger campaign, which aims to decrease hunger and poverty in Brazil. The campaign's start-ing point was ensuring that every family in the country had a meal three times a day and was inspired by Lula's own impoverished childhood and the frequent hunger he experienced. 'The first time I ate bread was at seven years old,' he told me. 'We lived on cassava. My parents were penniless.'

When he became president he decided to work with his ministers to fulfil as many of the objectives of his campaign as possible, asking them to constantly consider how the laws, policies and actions they proposed would work towards eradicating hunger in the country.

Today the Zero Hunger programme benefits over twelve million families, a quarter of Brazil's population. As one of the world's larg-est anti-poverty programmes after China's, it provides conditional direct-cash transfers to families to help reduce short-term pov-erty, and places an obligation on parents to put their children in school and to get them vaccinated.

Through these measures, poverty in Brazil fell by 27 per cent dur-ing Lula's administration. He also sought to carve out a place for Brazil in the world economy, recognising the increasingly prominent role of developing nations in manufacturing, innovation and trade. With China establishing itself as the world's factory and India as its technological capital, Brazil aspired to be the world's farm. Special credit lines were granted to small farmers, and they were given access to seed, finance, water, land and fertilisers. To ensure that farmers made a profit from their yields, Lula lobbied congress to pass a bill obliging local governments to buy at least 30 per cent of all farmers' produce.

He then linked his farming initiative to the government's school-feeding programme, boosting farmers' incomes and providing them with vital access to markets. The immediate impact, however, was an improvement in health, education and nutrition for Brazil's poor and hungry children.

Altogether, the harvests from rural farmers ended up accounting for 70 per cent of the country's food production, creating more value per hectare on Brazil's farmable land than their industrial counterparts. The surge of jobs in the farming industry consequently led to growth in manufacturing as well, particularly in the production of tractors for small farmers.

While Lula massively improved the living conditions of millions of Brazilians, no doubt saving the lives of many in the process, he is the first to admit that he was not a perfect leader and that he made many mistakes. He has been criticised for his failure to implement a more radical agrarian reform programme, his inability to transform a historically crooked and shady electoral system, and for not being tougher on corrupt senior comrades from his Workers' Party.

The continued infiltration of neoliberal capitalism into the economic policies of developing countries also occurred under Lula's watch and those of Dmitry Medvedev, Manmohan Singh and Hu Jintao, the respective leaders of Russia, India and China when the BRIC group was established in 2009. South Africa joined the association in 2010 and it became known as BRICS (the 'S' at the end of the term standing for South Africa). Its focus has been on improving the global economic situation for BRICS members, reforming financial institutions such as the IMF and World Bank, becoming more involved in global affairs and promoting bilateral cooperation on the basis of non-interference, equality and mutual benefit. As of 2015, the five BRICS countries represent over 3.6 billion people or half of the world's population. The five nations have a combined nominal GDP of US$16.6 trillion, equivalent to approximately 20 per cent of the gross world product, and an estimated US$4 trillion in combined foreign reserves.[2]

The hegemony of neoliberalism continues to infiltrate the economic strategies and outlooks of developing nations. Instead of creating an alternative to the neoliberal dogma that governs world politics, BRICS countries are striving to assimilate into the system, to create a centre of power in the South and East to compete with the powerful one in the West. But in order to drive this agenda, the issues that plague their citizens – poverty, unemployment, climate change and disease – are continually overlooked. The prerogatives of the 1 per cent remain of paramount concern in this system.

How much BRICS countries threaten the status quo and how far they will go in building an alternative to the current world system is a question that only struggle on the ground can determine. But any notion that BRICS will advance more inclusivity and equality across socio-economic lines seems far-fetched. BRICS countries such as China and Russia have a reputation for autocratic rule and curtailing the civil liberties of their citizens, restricting funding of activist organisations and prohibiting media and internet freedom.

The impeachment of President Dilma Rousseff of Brazil in August 2016 for allegedly breaking budgetary laws is another example of how neoliberal practices undermine previously thriving but atypical government structures. It is indicative of the existence of a fundamental flaw in democratic political systems, the outcome of a capitalist trajectory carved out by economic elites seeking to control all governing systems and much of civil society.

In order to form a majority in congress, the Workers' Party gave in too often to the demands of older corrupt parties and adopted policies that conflicted with its socialist outlook. Its dependence on transnationals in the mining and construction sectors also compromised the party's loyalties to its constituents. And when these factions noticed how much of the state's resources were going to the poor through Lula's hunger campaign, they launched an offensive to discredit the leaders who, while not necessarily endorsing or supporting their activities, had enabled them.

Media conglomerates, controlled by six families linked to conservative parties, used Brazilians' growing unhappiness to advance an agenda against the administration, constantly highlighting legitimate grievances of the masses in the news. The government's implementation of an austerity programme that saw major cuts in education spending deepened divides and the discontent of the citizens, all of which undermined Rousseff's position as leader of the left-wing socialist Workers' Party.

In 2015, when I discussed the state of the party with one of its senior members, Olívio Dutra, a former mayor of Porto Alegre, he explained how certain changes in its philosophy have caused it to move astray from its original cause, which was to serve the people. The Workers' Party, he explained, was once 'an umbrella organisation; a coalition of intellectuals, liberation theologians, union militants, landless and urban movements' that worked hard to overthrow the military dictatorship that ruled Brazil for over two decades, from 1964 to 1985.

Today, however, 'the institutionalisation of the PT has removed the organic connection with the people. Our goal has become winning power, in the towns, cities and nationally,' Dutra reflected. '*We have become bureaucratic and alienated from our mass base, with the people only mobilised when an election is being held.*' (Italics mine.)

The historical mission that defined the Workers' Party, a commitment to creating systemic change in tyrannical power structures, has been replaced with the need to hold on to power and wealth.

The similarities between this movement for the people and that of South Africa's African National Congress are striking.

Although the lives of many people in Brazil have improved since the Workers' Party came to power, the country still faces the age-old dilemma of rampant poverty among its majority who live in overpopulated favelas lacking basic services, and who depend on short-term casual jobs to get by on a day-to-day basis. They have refrigerators and televisions, but they have never escaped the deprivation and hardship that defines every one of their decisions and encounters, and every aspect of their daily existence. Austerity programmes will continue to hinder their progress as they are made to pay for an economic crisis in which they played no part, while the rich receive bailouts and enough tax breaks to help them cause another crisis in the future.

The 2013 demonstrations against Brazil's hosting of the FIFA World Cup – when hundreds of thousands of the country's youth took to the streets condemning the wasteful expenditure on stadiums – were one manifestation of the public's growing frustration with their government's apathy.

While they were trapped in a seemingly endless cycle of hardship and degradation, their leaders were able to source enough wealth to host a month-long sporting tournament that consumed billions in public funding.

The event serves as an important lesson to political elites in Brazil and South Africa, which hosted the FIFA World Cup in 2010. If we can build world-class stadiums to entertain a few tourists, why can't we deliver water, toilets, textbooks and electricity to our citizens? Surely our people deserve the 'FIFA-quality education, FIFA-quality health and FIFA-quality public transport' that the Brazilian protestors demanded?

There has been a blatant and disastrous move away from social justice as the primary ambition of what were once collectivist democratic political parties. When I think back to the early nineties and the robust debates between COSATU and the Brazilian trade union federation, Central Única dos Trabalhadores (Unified Workers' Central, CUT), the objective that always remained at the centre of our philosophy, regardless of any other differences we might have had, was the needs of the workers, the poor and the marginalised. CUT's alliances with the Workers' Party in Brazil and COSATU's with the ANC in South Africa were based on concrete programmes ˙ and policy objectives that fulfilled our aims for our people. We came from the same cloth of militant social unionism that obtained its power from its independence from the politics of others.

Social justice movements do not work this way today. *Many organisations that are set up to represent the invisible and the marginalised operate in silos and do not challenge the system.* Disconnected from their members, the priorities unions adopt are those of their more powerful political allies, which generally only serve the interests of a minority.

This was not the vision for the South–South solidarity during the height of the social justice struggle four decades ago. Our goal was to build an alternative political centre that was distinctly anti-colonial and anti-imperialist, and that would challenge the hegemonic neoliberal thinking of Europe and the United States. It was for a worker-centred alternative to capitalism and the Washington Consensus following what we knew would be its eventual decline.

None of this happened. And South Africa, Brazil and many other countries are still in need of dynamic structural reform of their political, social and economic institutions. Dutra agrees with this, believing that rising discontent among the Brazilian masses will continue if there is not a radical commitment to 'structural agrarian, political, tax education and urban planning reform in Brazil. This was the project we set out to achieve when we launched the PT. We cannot just focus on GDP growth. It has to be sustainable and socially inclusive. Otherwise it leads to rising inequality and social instability. Then the people have a right to rise up and condemn their government.'

Listening to these instructive voices from Brazil, or watching as millions around the world protest on the streets, I am struck once again by the arrogance of politicians who cause such unrest. I share the frustration that the marginalised have with officials who were elected to serve our interests and not to ignore our attempts to speak out when they fail. These are the events that remind me of what it means to be a servant leader, and how desperately in need we are of more individuals willing to carry the burden – and honour – of campaigning for social justice.

The social leader listens to the desperate pleas of the poor and carries their issues over to public discourse, giving them a voice where before no one had been willing to listen.

Servant leaders perform their duties in the spirit of service and with personal and political integrity. They accept that the buck stops at their offices of president, minister, premier, CEO, NGO head and union leader. A real servant leader *never* sees public service as an opportunity for self-enrichment.

A challenge in any social struggle is inspiring confidence in the people you are serving. You have to rise above their limitations and help them shape the futures they desire for themselves and their families. Anything less than this and you are merely replicating the failed development theories and practices of the past. Hope is a gift that only hard work and participation can build on.

11

The Power of the People

W HENEVER I AM asked about how I occupy my time
now that I am no longer with the union movement and in
government, I often feel loath to admit that I work (albeit as a volunteer) in the development space. The admission makes me cringe
because I have become more aware of the inherent dysfunction
that exists in the development sector's bureaucratic practices.

I am not so cynical that I cannot perceive what gains can be made
from partnerships between like-minded individuals and organisations. However, I do believe that an over-reliance on consultants
and technocrats who provide technical solutions to social issues
inhibit the struggle for social justice. Development activism has been
reduced to a set of disparate and fragmented projects that keep their
members in silos, isolated from the people they are supposed to be
rescuing from impoverishment and inequality. Instead of going out
into the field where they can meet and converse with their care base,
they attend conferences armed with flash drives that reiterate the
reasons for global poverty and war. All paths to change move towards
beseeching rich donors for aid, resulting in a dependence on handouts from bean-counter operatives often based in Western capitals.

While charitable endeavours form a façade for many activities
in the development space, in reality the sector is nothing more than

an attractive career destination for individuals hoping to travel to exotic locations, or to meet powerful or wealthy contacts.

For myself, however, working in the development sector has allowed me to witness first-hand some of the many strides being made by communities around the world as they try to foster their own growth and wealth. The lessons I learnt from these experiences have influenced and even transformed my participation in community development in South Africa, uncovering pathways on which older models of organisation have been renounced and new ones, while still mindful of historical and situational context, have been configured. Of course there can never be a one-size-fits-all solution to any social issue, but I am convinced that these communities are offering new ways for creating an alternative and more inclusive vision of the future – one that values the importance of socially useful livelihoods before dependence on government structures and donors.

In such a framework, communities produce the goods and services that will meet the needs of *their* people. It requires them to build their own asset base, which includes land and property, as well as communal institutions such as schools, clinics and establishments for food production. By working together, the members of these communities achieve a sense of solidarity with one another and are able to approach various social problems and issues in an ethical and peaceful manner. Checks and balances are carried out through peer pressure and through discussion and rapport.

While I am making no promises in the coming pages, I do think they offer viable solutions and potential ideas for activists seeking to make a difference in their communities and for those wishing to return to the basics of communal living and older, more inclusive ideas of wealth. The following examples are only shadows of what is possible. They need further work and input to be implemented on a grander scale.

Let's get started.

In May 2012 I visited the small tribal village of Araku in Andhra Pradesh, a populous state of over eighty million in the south of India.

My great-grandmother Angamma was born in a village like this more than 150 years ago, before she was forced as a young woman to leave on an old slave ship for a country she knew nothing about. During the journey she met my great-grandfather, the hope and love she gained from this encounter helping her to rediscover her humanity on a ship that treated her as a tradeable commodity. When she arrived in South Africa, she worked as an indentured labourer on a sugar plantation outside the port city of Durban, where I was born. In 1981 I visited the site in India where both her body and soul were abused. I remember feeling pride and humility at the courage she displayed during what must have been a traumatic experience.

Sitting in a hut in Araku in 2012, looking out at the lush green vegetation of the area, my thoughts travelled to Angamma's journey and how it initiated a series of events that would lead to my birth.

I wondered about what would result from my own journey in India, whether I would learn anything from the Naandi Foundation, a social enterprise that works in the area with the aim of eradicating poverty through innovative community-based solutions. Established in 1998, the foundation operates in fifteen states in India and has assisted over five million people in various initiatives, including the delivery of warm lunches to a million schoolchildren. In Araku, Naandi has succeeded in providing the villagers with safe drinking water, school feeding for children, livelihoods for small farmers, jobs for the youth, and targeted support for girls to receive a quality education. During my visit to the village, I realised how relevant its situation is to that of numerous communities in Africa. In fact, there is so much of Araku that is relevant to all developing countries.

Similar to the Khoisan in South Africa or the First Nations in North and South America, indigenous tribes in Indian villages such as Araku are the poorest of marginalised communities. Public investment in rural areas is at best minuscule. For a populous area like

Andhra Pradesh, where the indigenous people are listed in the constitution as 'scheduled classes', this has resulted in widespread impoverishment and destitution. Their moniker as the 'invisible people' of India has been rightfully, and tragically, earned.

I asked Manoj Kumar, the energetic CEO of Naandi, why he started working in Araku, a region so isolated from the rest of India. Kumar explained how this was precisely the reason for the organisation's presence in the village. '[Araku] was chosen for its remote location, in which there was a Maoist insurgency led by the Naxalites, against government. There was an absence of NGO presence and abysmally low indices in maternal and infant mortality and school enrolment, especially for girls.'

Low school attendance by girls is a common phenomenon in the developing world, including Africa, as cultural beliefs usually persuade parents not to invest in their daughters' schooling. Many girls are married off at a young age, while female infanticide is also prevalent in India.

When Naandi was founded in 1998 it piloted a programme for female education in Indian villages, working with corporate donors and government to create bursaries that would help girls remain in school. Naandi organisers had detailed conversations with parents explaining to them why it was important for their daughters to finish school, which would allow them to attend university and eventually get their own jobs.

A few years after the bursary scheme was implemented, the number of teenage pregnancies in the village plummeted. It seems that the girls in Araku felt like they had more control of their bodies and their futures. Before Naandi brought water and toilets to the village, many had to miss school every month when they were menstruating.

The results of the education programme gave Kumar hope that even more could be done to make Araku a thriving, successful community. 'We felt if we can crack Araku, we can solve poverty anywhere in the world. We thought we would bring development to Araku.'

But it was Kumar's description of Naandi's work with local farmers that really made an impact on me. Before carrying out any initiatives to transform the local farming industry, Naandi volunteers first had a discussion with farmers to find out what they hoped to get out of the organisation's input.

'We realised that the farmers knew the land better than us,' Kumar explained. 'So together we built an army of "barefoot development change agents" by training Adivasi [tribal] farmers as our team of trainers in their own fields. Now they can teach our staff about development.'

I felt as if I had been hit on the head with a rock. Imagine that: asking the community that you were professing to 'help' what it was that they actually needed.

This was my Newton moment, the eureka I had been searching for. It is what COSATU had done on the factory floor and the framework I would adopt in my own attempts to create change in South African communities. Once again, the union model I had always valued so highly was proving its worth in community organising.

Naandi's work in Araku has seen massive gains since it initiated its first programme in the village in 2001. This was a school-building initiative, as Araku's children had studied under trees before Naandi helped the community construct its first school with sticks, straw and mud walls. In three years, and through collaboration with both the community and the government, Naandi built 425 schools in Araku, ensuring that almost all the village's children were in school.

Kumar's work on improving education in Araku attracted the notice of Uwe Gustafsson, a Canadian linguist who had been working in these villages for thirty-five years on various literacy programmes and on codifying tribal dialects. During a routine inspection of the new schools in August 2002, Kumar came across

Gustafsson, who voiced his admiration for Naandi's efforts at improving education in Araku. Then he said, 'I wish you would do the same for landless peasants who have an acre of leased land from government to grow coffee, but whose lands are unproductive because they lack the skills and tools of agriculture.'

Naandi took up the challenge, establishing a cooperative of farmers who produced fair-trade coffee and black pepper through biodynamic agriculture. Before this, farmers had been earning one dollar for a kilogram of coffee. But after being trained in organic farming, learning to make natural fertiliser from cow dung and to process the coffee beans according to their quality, Araku farmers transformed their produce into goods that a wider, international market could appreciate. They now have organic certification for their produce and negotiated access to global markets, and have been able to increase their incomes to an average of five dollars per kilogram of coffee.

What began as an organisation of one thousand farmers has grown into the largest tribal farm cooperative in India. Over 100 000 farmers participate in the scheme and more than 26 000 acres of land in Andhra Pradesh have been allocated for food gardens in hundreds of villages. During my visit I met the board of farmers that oversaw the development of the initiative, all confident, focused leaders who were proud of their achievements. They showed me training manuals with pictures of the farming techniques that were used to grow organic produce, and proudly took me through their detailed farming records. They also showed me the geographic information system that captures the precise boundaries of their farms and provides proof of their legal title to the land.

These farming initiatives have helped a large number of Araku residents obtain a steady source of income, widening access for farmers and their families to education, medical care, better food sources, nutrition and fresh water. It is also a completely circular, fully sustainable community enterprise.

For David Hogg, one of Naandi's organic-farming gurus, sustainable organic agriculture in a community can only originate through a 'social transformation'. But when this transformation occurs, the effects are far-reaching, advantageous both to farmers and their customers, who appreciate the health benefits of organic produce and become loyal customers to those who farm it.

Organic farming is good for the environment too, as it shuns modern farming methods that use harmful chemicals for crop production. 'Our soil is sacred,' Hogg says. 'We cannot allow our planet to be poisoned any longer by insecticides, herbicides [and] chemical fertilisers ... that destroys local biodiversity and displaces and undermines the balanced diets of many local communities.'

Africa has nearly 60 per cent of the earth's remaining uncultivated arable land. As commercial agriculture continues to destroy soil quality and pollute waters in other countries because of chemical dependency, African terrain has become increasingly popular for farming produce for overseas markets. Major corporations and foreign governments lease or buy huge tracts of land in Africa, planting food here to feed only their populations. For Africans, whose farmers have limited access to land in their own countries, this means higher food prices and the movement of our wealth once again to overseas economies. This also impacts the diversity and health of the plants that farmers in Africa grow, Hogg explains, as 'the stranglehold of large transnationals on seed production and the introduction of genetically modified crops will deepen the burden of disease and rob communities of their seed sovereignty'.

Helping rural communities regain control of their land is something I feel passionately about. For too long American multinationals like Monsanto have dominated market share in the agricultural industry and seed production, robbing us of our right to healthy organic-grown food by proliferating the spread of genetically modified products.

The race by such corporations to produce larger quantities of food for profit rather than to promote healthy living has resulted in the creation and spread of foods that are questionable in origin or harmful to our health. Our food – infused with toxic chemicals, or over-processed and full of sugar, salt and fat – is making us ill. It is estimated that two-thirds of our disease burden is caused by bad diet. It is imperative that we start seeing our seed as our life. It is the source of the nourishment we give to our bodies and a gift from nature that we should treasure. This is our God-given birth right, and not something that should be owned or commodified. We should not be tampering with it.

Naandi has also begun using carbon credits to fund the planting of seven million organic mango trees in Andhra Pradesh. This project was the start of a broader effort to help local communities become food secure by providing them with resources to plant their own vegetable gardens and earn an income from exporting surplus produce to cities.

The outcome of the initiative demonstrates one essential point: that sustainable development for rural communities actually exists. It is the result of meticulous and careful planning by communities to create their own livelihoods. COSATU succeeded in organising socially conscious, dedicated workers, not by 'selling' politics, but around the appealing prospect of higher wages. We did this by improving employees' working conditions and their experiences on the shop floor, building their confidence in the process so that they would be prepared to fight their own battles in future. As both the Araku and COSATU models indicate, organisational success arises through a combination of hard work, disciplined commitment, respect and empathy, and solidarity and cooperation.

In Araku, villagers have learnt to be enterprising when it comes to obtaining highly needed resources for their community. Garam Kumbo, chairman of the Araku Coffee Cooperative, has benefited enough from Naandi's work in the village that he was able to pay for both his son and daughter to attend university, and even to buy an ambulance for the community. The system of sharing and solidarity that Naandi has encouraged in Araku makes sense to the villagers: to get something back from your community, every single member has to put something into it.

Naandi's water-treatment programme, which provides half a million rural people with safe drinking water, is another initiative that has been driven and sustained by communities. In one of the villages in Araku, the water system had collapsed. Residents had been pestering government officials for months to have it fixed, but nothing came from their pleas. Eventually, they decided to do something about it themselves, collecting enough money to contribute to half of the repair costs while the co-op gave the rest. But although they were looking forward to having clean water again, the villagers were not prepared to sit back and wait for their water system to break down again. Instead, they planned to join up with nearby villages and march on government offices to protest the water issue.

The next time a political party showed up to ask for their votes, they would face some serious questions. Araku was not a powerless community any more. They had already taken pains to ensure that teachers began arriving for their lessons on time as many had not done so in the past. Those who refused to comply were promptly removed from their posts. The villagers were using their power in every societal sphere that was of benefit to their community – from water and health to food and education.

The solidarity between villagers in communities in Andhra Pradesh is admirable, and somewhat intimidating. In Mattam Korthur, a village situated close to Araku, residents have built a place for community meetings under a tree and they bestowed on me the honour of inaugurating it, which I gratefully accepted.

To my untrained eye, the village looked like a successful, thriving place. Houses were renovated, and the children were immaculately dressed and well disciplined when I spoke to them at their school. They were excited about meeting someone from a distant country, and although they did not really know where South Africa was, they had heard of Mandela. He is the Mahatma Gandhi of Africa, they asserted.

Gandhi would no doubt have been proud to see the progress that tiny villages like these have made in spite of all the challenges they face. He was not interested simply in exchanging the rule of white sahibs for rule by brown sahibs; he wanted the Indian government to surrender much of its power to local villages.

For Gandhi, the spirit and soul of India rested in village communities. 'The true India,' he averred, 'is to be found not in its few cities, but in its seven hundred thousand villages. If the villages perish, India will perish too.'

His vision of a free India was not a nation-state but a confederation of self-governing, self-reliant individuals residing in village communities and deriving their livelihood from their homesteads. This is a strategy for community life that is as relevant today in a rapidly urbanising world as it was during Gandhi's time. As poor and vulnerable communities confront the effects of climate change and overpopulation, community solidarity and sustainability are their incubators against future conflicts arising from these issues.

Of course, no amount of solidarity and unity can accomplish a complete end to all conflict in communities. But they do serve as suitable weapons against those who instigate it. When I returned to Araku, I asked the villagers at a community meeting what the main problems were that confronted them.

A young woman called Sumoni stood up and said: 'We have banned alcohol in our village. It is an evil drug that destroys our families and breaks our community spirit.'

The majority of attendees applauded Sumoni's pronouncement. I did the same. But there were some men who seemed rather sullen about this fact. It did not help their argument that a drunk man from another village wandered into the meeting at one point and had to be thrown out. Having personally witnessed what alcohol abuse does to families in South African communities, a consequence of poverty, joblessness and hopelessness, I was not surprised at the stance that Araku had taken towards the substance. Men in particular turn to drinking as an escape, and violence against women and children is usually the outcome of their addiction. Community development is essential for creating long-term solutions for crime prevention, which include investment in social and cultural activities that offer alternative forms of entertainment to alcohol consumption.

In Araku, maintaining a record of activities and processes that promote peace and functionality in the village is integral for ensuring their continued promulgation. Tranadh, a thirty-eight-year-old mother of two children, is a village committee volunteer whose job it is to monitor knowledge transfer, such as the rules of the village and its elections and financial transactions. She was well trained in her duties and showed pride in the knowledge she had gained as a volunteer. She was also grateful for what it would mean for her children.

'My children will have a better life,' Tranadh explained. 'They will have a better education. I am learning how to look after their health. Naandi showed me that women are an equal part of the community.'

This was probably one of the most effective results of Naandi's work in rural communities – educating traditional societies to respect women's rights and to value the crucial role that mothers, sisters and daughters play in every community. Now this has become the Araku way.

To me, Araku has proved itself as a successful model of community organisation and development. I thought that perhaps I could help create something similar in my own country, although I was not entirely sure at this point whether I could. For all the similarities between India and South Africa, there are also many more differences. I did not want to impose a structure of what I believed to be a successful community on a South African village that shared no similar experiences with those in India. I wanted to work with people the way Naandi did, to create partnerships with communities and the people who shared my ambition of co-creating success and building from below.

Luckily we live in a big world. There was still more to see, and much more to learn.

12

The World
in Microcosm

THE POVERTY IN Bangladesh is glaring. As one of the world's
poorest countries, there are no visible enclaves of sheltered
privilege the likes of which South Africans or Brazilians are used to.
Twice as dense as India and China, Bangladesh can be considered
one of the most populous, chock-a-block nations on the planet.
Teeming masses of humanity seem to pour out of every space
and corner in the country, its roads a gridlock of rickshaw pullers,
plush 4×4s, battered buses and lumbering, overladen lorries from
a bygone era. Here, driving is not for the faint-hearted.

Much of Bangladesh's current plight can be attributed to the
Bangladesh Liberation War of 1971, when Bengali nationalists rose
up against Pakistan's authoritarian rule of their country, formerly
part of Pakistan's eastern territory. Up to one and half million
Bangladeshis are estimated to have died in the civil war that followed, while 200 000 to 400 000 Bangladeshi women were raped in
a strategy of genocidal rape by Pakistan's army of occupation.

Bangladesh's institutional and intellectual classes were also
largely destroyed in the massacre. Although the country eventually
won independence, the war left it devastated and the majority of its

citizens impoverished. In 1975, following the assassination of Sheikh Mujibur Rahman, the Bangladesh republic's first prime minister and the man regarded as the country's founding father, the country slid into further turmoil.

But when I visited Bangladesh in 2013 it had already achieved a number of the UN's Millennium Development Goals, which gave nations targets for addressing poverty, human rights issues and disease. Some of the goals realised by Bangladesh include the reduction of poverty by half, a massive fall in its child and maternal mortality rates, and an almost universal enrolment of girls in school. Between 1990 and 2010, life expectancy in Bangladesh rose ten years, from fifty-nine to sixty-nine years.

These figures are extraordinary, and I was eager to find out just how Bangladesh had accomplished this.

My first visit was to Korail, a crowded urban slum in Dhaka, Bangladesh's capital, where the streets are narrow, perforated with gaping, open gutters and crammed with human beings. Within this maze of traders, selling everything from food and airtime to medicine and health services, I had to find the area's Delivery Centre, one of numerous childbirth facilities scattered throughout the country's squatter camps and villages as part of a healthcare initiative for mothers and children by the Bangladesh Rural Advancement Committee (BRAC).

Much of the societal progress that Bangladesh has made in recent years is due to BRAC, the largest non-governmental organisation in the world which was founded in 1972 by Sir Fazle Hasan Abed, a social worker, and its sister organisation, the Grameen Bank, set up in 1976 by Professor Muhammad Yunus, a Nobel Prize–winning economist who has been fighting poverty for years.

With over eight million members, BRAC's projects impact an estimated 120 million people, and a further six million in the urban slums. Given that Bangladesh's population in 2016 was 163 million people, BRAC's scale of community development is absolutely astonishing.

When I arrived at the Delivery Centre, the heat was rising, the air extremely humid. Outside the centre stood neat rows of sandals belonging to people who were inside. I really admire this tradition; it displays respect for the home and keeps it clean and free of disease. I entered a squashed space full of women in colourful garb. They were there for a meeting of the Mothers' Club, an organisation of healthcare volunteers that assists pregnant and lactating women. The volunteers were known as *shasthya sebika*s ('village women'), and there were close to 100 000 of them in BRAC. During their review of their week's activities, I listened carefully, thinking of areas in South Africa where people die regularly of preventable diseases and children are visibly affected by malnutrition.

As the Mothers' Club discussed their goals and duties, I was once again reminded of my interactions with communities as a union organiser. These women were like shop stewards in the factories who knew everything that happened in their villages because they lived there. Mothers' Club volunteers were informed about every woman who was pregnant, lactating or raising a young child, and it did not matter to them whether she fell under the care of another volunteer.

One of the *shasthya sebika*s, a woman named Kohinoor, explained to me what her job entails. 'I live here in the slum,' she said. 'I was trained. I visit ten households a day. I monitor all mothers and children and track progress of pregnant mothers. We bring the mothers to the central delivery centre to receive regular education. Each mother has a book detailing [her] progress, but also providing simple information about the dos and don'ts during her pregnancy. I spend time with the husbands, educating them about pregnancy and also involving them as fathers.'

The Mothers' Club is an on-the-ground surveillance system, and every one of its procedures has been standardised and is understood in intricate detail by volunteers. If a complication arises, a local midwife, a *shasthya sebika* or her supervisor, a *shasthya kormi*, are a phone call away and available within minutes. The logistics chain of the organisation is seamless. A rickshaw ambulance, navigating Korail's narrow rutted streets, takes the expectant mother to the main street where a vehicular ambulance waits and she is then driven to the local hospital, which has already been alerted to her approaching arrival. Like many brilliant strategies, this referral system is both elaborate and simple. After being led through the process, I understood immediately why maternal and infant mortality rates had fallen so drastically. Internal haemorrhaging, a scourge of maternal mortality, has decreased too, and 90 per cent of mothers breastfeed their child in the first hour.

Just as it was with Naandi in Araku, women's empowerment was at the centre of BRAC's successful developmental strategy in Korail. Mothers form its cornerstone, which emphasises how much they are valued in society, while 70 per cent of its employees are women.

Simplicity. System. Commitment. Standardisation.

The correct process to follow when organising a community was beginning to take shape for me. Like all systems, it has to be built from below, by people who recognise the value it will add to their lives.

The day after my meeting with the Mothers' Club, I visited another village where I met with more *shasthya sebikas*. I wanted to interrogate their model further and understand it at a village level. How did it work at scale, I asked?

One of the supervisors, Sumaya, told me how her own experiences informed her decision to join the Mothers' Club. 'I was a mother,' she said. 'I saw the value of the education I received. I applied and was selected. After my training, I was allocated an area to work. My job was to monitor and educate the pregnant mothers and also the families, especially their husbands. I also teach women about their rights, family planning, the law and justice.'

I asked whether the volunteers noted any resistance or antagonism from husbands to their efforts. There was an excited response.

'Yes, at first,' Sumaya said. 'But our children were always sick. Now they are healthier. We showed that some of our cultural practices were not right for the child or the mother. For example, some mothers did not breastfeed in the first hour because they thought it was bad for the child. Now 90 per cent breastfeed in an hour and exclusive breastfeeding is above 65 per cent for the first six months. And we are finally respected by our husbands and our community. We have dignity.'

This is a valuable lesson for those seeking to create organisational strategies in rural or traditional communities. Cultural norms should always be respected and integrated into plans. At the same time, organisers should be aware of harmful cultural practices that categorically violate human rights. While in Bangladesh, I had a discussion with Professor Muhammad Yunus about sexist cultural and tribal traditions. Yunus spoke strongly against all 'cultural practices, patriarchy and traditions that are harmful to the rights of women ... [and] obsolete' in the twenty-first century. In Yunus's forceful terms, these traditions 'should be thrown into the rubbish bin' – a sentiment I share wholeheartedly.

During my meeting with the *shasthya sebikas*, I noticed that they were all carrying black leather bags. I asked Sumaya to show me what was inside. She opened hers to reveal a store of over-the-counter medicines such as dehydration fluid, micronutrient sprinkles, painkillers and iron tablets, which the volunteers have been trained to dispense correctly; as well as sanitary pads, female contraception and condoms. For those who received advanced training, there were eye tests – the most expensive costing less than $2 – and treatment for hypertension. BRAC has accredited twenty-two medical and health products, and the *shasthya sebikas* earn a percentage of each item sold. Just like Naandi's farming scheme, the Mothers' Club is a fully sustaining model of social entrepreneurship with a conscience of service at its core. It is a source of inspiration for my work in South African communities.

With Sumaya as my guide, I next visited the home of Nurmahar, a new mother who was receiving advice and assistance from the Mothers' Club. Her house, a simple mud adobe structure, was spotless and proud. Nurmahar's baby, Turna, was seven months old and about to eat her first meal of solid food. Sumaya led the lesson. First, the mother has to wash her hands before making the baby's food, a simple dish of dhal lentils, fish, rice, green herbs and one teaspoon of soya bean oil mashed together in a measuring bowl. A sachet of micronutrients is then mixed into the food. Turna, uninterested in all the strangers in her house, swallowed her food happily, giggling and waving her hands wildly at her mother, eager for more.

BRAC's initiatives for educating mothers on pregnancy and child-care are saving the lives of thousands of children. *They are building community power and cohesion through systematic education and the co-creation of tools.* The Mothers' Club has standardised processes that are plugged in directly to BRAC's 'mother ship', ensuring that they are carried through on a closed loop that is constantly monitoring, evaluating and feeding back. Peer pressure from members, and not fear of the administration, keeps the mission and its disciples alive.

I asked Sir Fazle Hasan Abed how he introduced this kind of inclusive, functional bureaucracy into his organisation. His answer, by this point, should not be surprising. Abed emphasised that organisers should 'never be arrogant that we know everything. Even the best ideas fail in implementation. *We must learn to listen to the voices of the community.*' (Italics mine.)

Even a well-organised structure like BRAC can experience losses if it fails to incorporate this lesson into its philosophy. Abed described one project that BRAC had undertaken during the monsoon season in Bangladesh, when dysentery and diarrhoea are common among children, and which was at first met with great fanfare. The project followed a process of teaching mothers how to hydrate their children with a simple saline solution that they could make themselves with salt, sugar and water. 'But we failed,' Abed told me, 'because we did not bring the family, the husbands and the in-laws into the discussion.'

The primary ingredient missing from the solution? *Inclusion.* Lesson learnt.

BRAC provides an inspirational model for developmental organisations and groups, aspiring constantly to learn from its successes and failures and to adapt to new or changing circumstances in the communities in which it operates. BRAC embraces the notion that people are not bystanders in their own development, educating them and teaching them to think for themselves so that they can find success in the businesses or enterprises that BRAC helps them establish.

There is so much to learn in Bangladesh. Despite being a politically divided and fragile nation, it is united by its communities' determination to make their homes, and in the process their country, better places in which to live. Bangladeshi villages are frequently subject to tsunamis, cyclones, floods and drought; but this only fosters resilience among residents, making them less dependent on government and more dependent on themselves.

This is what community organising is about. *It does not seek to create communities of helpless or disillusioned individuals, but to inspire people to see the potential in themselves and others.* And once communities have been organised to believe in their capacity for change, it will not be very long before they begin organising change by themselves.

There have, however, been negatives to Bangladesh's socio-economic success. While girls are no longer excluded from education and can pursue their own careers, many of these jobs are in the garment industry, where the work is back-breaking and the conditions hazardous. More than four million workers, mostly girls, are employed in the industry, which has benefited from job losses in China as manufacturers move to locations with cheaper labour costs.

I travelled to the killing fields of Savar, a sub-district of Dhaka, where weeks before, on 24 April 2013, 1 127 garment workers had died when Rana Plaza, an eight-storey commercial building, collapsed, the deadliest clothing-factory tragedy in history. At the site of the building was a gaping hole in the ground. The torn ramparts of neighbouring buildings hung over the area like broken limbs. The entire scene had the haunting atmosphere of death.

On Dhaka's outskirts is the local hospital where survivors were taken. It is a care facility for the physically challenged and was already overcrowded. There are fans in every room in the wards, but they bring little relief.

One of the survivors I spoke to was Rozina, who worked as a sewing-machine operator in the factory. Her sister, who was employed by the same firm, worked with her on the third floor.

Rozina described to me her experience of the building's collapse. 'I heard a huge bang,' she recalled. 'The roof collapsed. The concrete beam struck me. I could not see my sister. My head hit the sewing machine. I felt the steel rods pierce my back. The table had fallen on my hand, crushing it.'

'I felt I had died,' she said.

For the whole of that day Rozina lay in the same spot where she had fallen. She could hear rescuers searching for survivors but she was not able to call to them. It was only the next day that she was found, when rescuers spotted her through a small hole in the rubble. She had been trapped down there for forty-eight hours and could feel the life leaving her. But the rescuers could not get her out because her hand was trapped underneath some stone and it was too mangled for her to remove it by herself.

That was when the rescuers suggested she cut off her hand so they could pull her out. 'It was the only hope,' Rozina explained to me. 'I took the hacksaw and began cutting. But I was too weak to cut through the bone.'

Eventually, after sixty-one hours of 'hell', Rozina was rescued from the collapsed building. She remembers losing consciousness 'as I was pulled out and the tendons and cartilage [of my hand] ripped'.

The trauma of this experience will stay with her forever, the death of her sister and the loss of her hand constant reminders of what that factory has taken from her. 'I am alive but my dreams are shattered,' she said, pointing to the stump to which her hand had been attached.

Rozina's story is one that has been repeated countless times in Bangladesh and other developing countries where little concern is shown for the working conditions of factory labourers. Only days before the collapse, Rana Plaza, owned by a politically connected businessman, was visited by government building inspectors who said that the building should be closed and evacuated. We know this never happened.

When Rozina finished her account, Nazma Akhter, the president of the Union of Garment Workers Association, turned to me and said, 'We need people in the West to understand that there is nothing free. When you buy cheap clothing or buy one and get one free, realise that nothing is free. Someone has to pay. Here, it is the workers with their lives. Our lives are cheap.'

But even building collapses and loss of life will do very little to improve workers' conditions in the factories. There is no reason to make workers' lives easier if producing garments for indifferent consumers remains this cheap. Bangladesh is one of the world's largest exporters of clothing, second only to China, making the country's textile industry the principal source of its foreign-exchange earnings. 'We have a long struggle ahead,' Akhter told me. 'We need these jobs, but we must stop the killing. We need the bosses to understand that we are human beings who have basic human rights. This should not have happened if our unions were recognised and we had the right channels to raise our grievances.'

I had seen this before in apartheid South Africa and other societies hit by economic and social crises. In such contexts, unions are usually the first targets of governments attempting to control a tenuous political situation. But this opens workers up to abuses by their employers and terrible working conditions.

I can feel the anger rising again – the same anger that coursed through me when I experienced apartheid injustices.

We see it flashed across our TV screens constantly. Unrest in Turkey, India, South Africa, Brazil. The people I meet, the forgotten of society, are enraged. They feel alienated from their leaders, who choose not to hear their citizens proclaim, 'We do not trust our leaders. They serve the interests of the rich. Democracy is on sale to the highest bidder. We are only needed when they want our votes.'

Bangladesh has been wounded by the tragedy in Savar, the workers in the sweatshops of Rana Plaza the sacrificial victims of global human greed and consumerism. These are the soldiers at the front line of a brutal war for low costs and massive profits.

What matters are the people at the end of the line of production, the millions of Western shoppers and their favourite brands: Benetton and Nike, Gap and J. Crew. Glitzy advertising campaigns and beautiful celebrities feed this frenzy for consumption, telling their customers to identify with trademarks and slogans of material goods while the people who make them are disregarded even in their own countries.

The Rana Plaza disaster should have been a wake-up call for us as consumers.

We should demand as consumers that global brands be held to account for the slave-labour conditions in which our clothes are made every day. This is a system we were supposed to have abolished nearly two centuries ago.

As consumers, we have to begin purchasing goods and products with a conscience. We need to ask ourselves whether what we have bought was made by slaves or free human beings, whether any lives were lost or bodies maimed for our favourite pair of sneakers or the latest cellphone we so desperately want. As jobs become increasingly automated and robotics takes over factory production, we have to ensure that the people who still work in these places are not treated like robots either.

Neoliberalism is not a religion, although it attempts to validate trickle-down economics and consumerism as the inevitable order of things – the reason that people are treated like things and things like people. Our minds have been colonised by these ideas, brainwashed into believing that they constitute actual science, when real science has painted a detailed picture of the disasters that have occurred in this system: climate change, hunger, economic crises, humanitarian disasters and widespread inequality.

These issues underline a present and future loss not only of planetary and economic resources, but of spiritual values too. It is time for labour organisations, civil society, social movements, progressive governments and businesses to restore ideas of equality and democracy to the popular mindset, to shape and elaborate a new paradigm of sustainable growth that emphasises the worth of every human being. Anything else, and the indictment that future generations will place on us will not only be lasting, but well deserved.

13

Organising for a Planet

WITH THE INFILTRATION of neoliberal theory in world economic relations, and the subsequent rise of mass production and consumerism, humanity's demands on nature have become unsustainable, threatening our planet's ability to grow or maintain life. Pollution, climate change and a decline in natural resources are not only threatening to wipe out animal and plant species, but the survival of human beings is at stake too. In cities, carbon monoxide emissions from car exhaust fumes are primary causes of air pollution and respiratory diseases in inhabitants, while acid rain produced by dangerous particles in the air contaminates water supply and vegetation. People in rural areas have been greatly affected by global warming and hotter seasons, their water supply and food production diminishing as rivers and streams continue to dry up.

I witnessed the harmful effects of climate change on rural communities first-hand during a visit to Lake Turkana in northern Kenya in 2014. In Nanipi, a village situated close to the lake, Maria Akingol, one of the locals, showed me the receding shorelines of the waters, largely dried up owing to prolonged drought and dam building.

For desperately poor people like Maria who also have children to take care of, the diminishing fish stocks in the lake caused by saltier warmer water is a major threat to their livelihood. A lack of rain has stunted farming efforts in the village as well, Maria explained, the soil degraded and strewn with 'the whitened bones of animals that die in numbers because the rains are not coming as regularly as before. [Villagers] talk in hushed, fearful whispers of the wars over water and grazing land. Our children must go to Nairobi. It will be safer.'

Warmer weather and a subsequent depletion in resources is the cause of deepening instability in developing regions, where bad governance and tribal conflicts already restrict citizens' access to water, food and other resources. The movement of rural inhabitants to the cities generates further conflict over resources, as population pressure – particularly in the slums where the displaced are forced to reside – increases.

And yet these communities are not the ones responsible for the earth's growing ecological crisis. They have produced no carbon emissions. There are no fridges and air conditioners here, or extravagant yachts sailing on their waters. While city dwellers have access to food and clean water, the residents of villages like Nanipi have to eke out a living as pastoralists and fishermen, taking just enough from the earth to survive and feed their families and no more.

With the discovery of massive reserves of oil and underground water in the Turkana region in 2015, perhaps some positive change will come to the region and its inhabitants. This seems unlikely, however, given the stranglehold that governments have over profits and output owing to 'resource nationalism'.

Government and corporate exploitation of resources is the main instigator of environmental crises in areas that are rich in natural resources and fossil fuels, such as the Niger Delta in the south of Nigeria. The delta forms the heart of Nigeria's revenue stream, with 75 per cent of the country's export earnings coming from the region's oil reserves since 1975.[1] But decades of oil extraction has led to numerous environmental crises, including thousands of oil spills by the companies that operate in the region. The dominant corporation in the region is Royal Dutch Shell, the fourth largest company in the world. In 2014, oil companies reported a combined number of nearly 600 spills in Nigeria.[2] The burning or flaring of gas extracted from oil wells is also a major pollutant of the air, making the delta the single largest source of greenhouse gas emissions on the planet. The impact this has had on the environment and the region's ecosystem, as well as on the people who live there, is devastating to say the least.[3]

It was heartbreaking for me to see the damage that oil spillage and natural gas extraction have wreaked on the small village of Rumuekpe in Rivers State when I visited the area in 2014. It was like something out of Dante's *Inferno*, the ninth circle of hell. Gas flares can be spotted rising above the trees bordering the village, while the fumes make the air toxic and difficult to breathe. The heat and noise from the flares and machinery are unbearable too, adding to my sense of suffocation as I struggled to take in air. I cannot believe there are people who actually live there, but the locals told me they have no other choice. 'These are our ancestral lands,' they said. 'We have nowhere to go, while our children suffer respiratory problems, skin rashes and eye irritations.'

Nnimmo Bassey, executive director of the Health of Mother Earth Foundation (HOMEF), an ecological think tank, is my guide during this trip. He tells me that there are 200 flares burning across the Niger Delta at any given time, their fumes containing substances such as nitrogen oxides, benzene, toluene and xylene which are known to cause cancer. These pollutants affect communities as far away as two kilometres from the gas flares.

Gas extraction is the primary cause of acid rain, which has had a destructive impact on agriculture and fishing in the region – the major sources of livelihood for 90 per cent of Rumuekpe's inhabitants.[4] Of the nearly twenty-seven million people who live in the Niger Delta, an estimated 75 per cent rely on the environment for their livelihood, either by selling their produce or fishing or through subsistence living.[5] Oil extraction has led to the deep impoverishment of the Ogoni people and surrounding communities in the Delta.

But oil is supposed to be a windfall for a country, is it not? Should the wealth that has been made from Nigeria's oil supply not have transformed the country for the better? With its long history of anti-colonial activism, Nigeria should have been an example to oil-rich countries such as those in the Middle East, which exploit their citizens and despoil their environment for the benefit of their elites. Instead, some of the world's worst environmental and human rights abuses occur in Nigeria, committed by government and multinationals, who are their new oppressors.

Eric Doo, a chief from the Ogoniland community in Goi, provided me with a vivid and tragic account of the kind of damage that companies like Shell are inflicting on rural villages. An oil spill in Goi in October 2004 left the area devastated. There was palpable despair in Doo's voice as he recalled the town's formerly flourishing community and the beauty of its natural surroundings. Its fish ponds, mangrove forests and fruit trees were destroyed in a fire caused by the spillage. It took Shell nearly three years to begin cleaning up the ponds, but two months later, in August 2007, they were once again the site of an oil leak. Today there are no fish left in Goi's ponds and the town is deserted, a thick layer of crude covering its formerly beautiful terrain.

'This is Shell,' said Doo angrily. 'This is their legacy, and our hell. They have murdered our communities, killed our way of life. We have been here for generations; the remains of our ancestors now lie in these oil-soaked wastelands. And still they refuse to acknowledge what they have done ... All we want is for them to apologise; to say sorry for the damage they have caused. They are one of the richest companies in the world. Surely they can compensate us for our losses, help us rehabilitate our lands and recover from this disaster.'

It was only in June 2016 that the Nigerian government, in accordance with a plan devised by the United Nations Environment Programme (UNEP), launched a billion-dollar initiative to clean up Ogoniland and restore its swamps, forests, fishing ponds and creeks. However, it will take decades for the environment to recover its former glory. Shell in the meantime maintains that its efforts to clean the region have been substantial: 'The 15 Shell Petroleum Development Corporation (SPDC) joint venture sites specifically mentioned in the UNEP report have been reassessed, and where further remediation was required due to repollution incidents, such sites have been remediated and certified by regulators.'[6]

Years of lawsuits, false promises and further oil spills, and Shell, despite 'green washing' itself in the global media, still denies all responsibility for the harm it has done to Nigerian communities. Their prerogative is money and their defence pure denial, and they have the resources to continue avoiding liability by dragging out lawsuits and exploiting their economic power.

The governments who benefit from their business do nothing to impede or restrict their unscrupulous activities, while large international non-governmental organisations are too caught up in their own internal politics or with pedantic bureaucratic practices to offer any practical solutions.

Twenty years since the ground-breaking Earth Summit of 1992, which recognised the importance of 'sustainable development' and that 'industrialised countries should pay for the pollution generated through their growth', the world is still left without a substantive climate-change agreement. Donald Trump's election as president of the United States provides a further setback to any meaningful measures that have been taken by industrialised nations to reduce their emission of fossil fuels. In an effort to revive the US's diminishing coal industry, Trump – who has referred to climate change as a 'hoax' – is pledging to withdraw the US from the Paris climate accord, which is at least an acknowledgement by world leaders that global warming presents a serious threat to the planet and the lives of billions of people.

The trip to Nigeria was what did it for me. The waste and loss and destruction, instead of paralysing me, made me want to do something to give the land and its resources back to the people. They are the land's rightful owners, communities who tend to the earth with their hands and take only what it is prepared to give them.

On the other side of things are the corporations and governments. Those who cut down our trees, poach our animals and poison our air to feed the greed of an eternally hungry market of consumers. They are destroying big chunks of the natural world, as well as the habitats of species that billions depend on to survive.

In the last 540 million years there have been five mass extinctions on earth, in which at least 75 per cent of the planet's species were wiped out in a very short period of geological time. But now a sixth mass extinction is on its way, and this one is caused by us human beings.

The World Wide Fund for Nature's Living Planet Report provides an index that measures the status of decline of more than 10 000 mammals, birds, reptiles, amphibians and fish. Since 1970 their numbers have dropped by 52 per cent.[7]

If three-quarters of the earth's animals become extinct, we face the collapse of ecosystems which are important for our survival, including those in the oceans and rain forests. Any future technological innovations would likely be extremely expensive and benefit only a small number of people, mostly those who live in developed countries.

And yet appeals from scientists to engage in radical programmes for reducing carbon emissions have fallen on deaf ears. In the next century 20 to 30 per cent of plant and animal species face extinction if the earth continues to get warmer, and humans seem to believe it is their privilege to decide which of these species should live and which should die.

This should not be an us-versus-them prerogative. All species have a rightful place on this planet. Humans must begin looking at existence as occurring in one massive circle – the biosphere – and within that circle are millions of smaller circles that represent every species that currently survives on earth. It should alarm us that one of those small circles, the one occupied by humans, takes up 40 per cent of the entire massive circle. So as the planet's most dominant species, both in development and size, we should see it as our duty to care for all life that exists on it.

For as long as humans live, our survival and those of other species are mutually dependent on one another. Consider societies in regions such as the Niger Delta, which have become dysfunctional following the destruction of their natural environment. In the developing world, where there are no animals, plants and trees, there are no jobs, no food and no life. This would never be tolerated in Europe and America, which by now would have implemented measures to prevent the frequent occurrence of oil spills. Yet in Africa, governments expect their people – the majority of whom are poor – to not only endure continual pollution, but to live for years or even decades without access to food or clean water. New pipelines are set up in Nigeria, or plans for fracking in the Karoo are instigated, even though the companies approved to carry out these measures have revealed time and again their indifference to the plight of local populations and the environment. A shortage of money preventing governments from helping their people is one thing. But there is no excuse for the consistently destructive treatment of the environment. Gandhi once said, 'The world has enough for everyone's need, but not enough for everyone's greed.' Let us start appreciating and making use of what the earth has to offer; not continue to disregard its value for the fleeting worth of material goods.

Since record-keeping began, eleven of the last fifteen years have been the warmest on record. NASA reports that 2016 has broken all records.[8]

At the Earth Summit in Rio in 1992, world leaders recognised the tenuous state of the global environment. But it was only eight years later, on 29 January 2000, that the United Nations Educational, Scientific and Cultural Organization (UNESCO) and civil society organisations across a wide spectrum, representing tens of millions of people, adopted the Earth Charter as our point of departure for living in a just, sustainable and peaceful world. It begins:

> We stand at a critical moment in Earth's history, a time when humanity must choose its future ... We must join together to bring forth a sustainable global society founded on respect for nature, universal human rights, economic justice, and a culture of peace. Towards this end, it is imperative that we, the peoples of Earth, declare our responsibility to one another, to the greater community of life, and to future generations.

Almost twenty-five years later, and the earth is more vulnerable than ever, while people continue to engage in destructive conflicts and wars, inhibiting discourse and agreement in world relations when it is now needed most.

The Paris Agreement, signed in 2015 by 195 countries, seemed to be a victory for the planet and future generations. Taken with the UN Sustainable Development Goals, it presents a global agenda to end poverty and hunger by 2050, and to keep global warming below 2 degrees Celsius and preferably below 1.5 degrees. The latter will be achieved by abandoning all fossil fuels within this century.

World leaders are toasting what is believed to be the first 'truly universal' environmental agreement in history, but the facts say otherwise. According to an analysis by the UN Framework Convention on Climate Change, the pollution-reduction pledges made by countries ahead of the Paris talks will actually increase the world's temperature by 2.7 degrees Celsius by the year 2100.[9] This makes the entire agreement 'a fraud', according to former NASA scientist James Hansen, a leader in the global awareness campaign to fight climate change. 'It's just bullshit for them to say: "We'll have a 2 degrees Celsius warming target and then try to do a little better every five years,"' he says about the plans set forward in the accord.

In fact, if countries are to keep their promise to reduce fossil fuel emissions, they will have to leave 82 per cent of the world's coal underground, 50 per cent of its gas unburnt and a third of its oil reserves untouched. This is not happening, as more governments and corporations continue to invest large sums in searching for fossil fuel reserves.[10]

'More than half of the world's cities are at risk,' Hansen says.

We have heard it all before. As the earth gets warmer and the polar ice caps melt, sea levels will continue to rise until entire swathes of land are covered in water. The consequences will be devastating, and are almost unimaginable. Hansen stresses this point: 'The economic cost of a business-as-usual approach to emissions is incalculable. It will become questionable whether global governance will break down irretrievably.'

This might sound alarmist, but it is a theory that has been posited by some of the greatest minds currently studying the planet and attempting to understand its future. And, frankly, maybe it is time for people to start being alarmed. The knowledge that our planet is heading towards an avoidable and completely human-made end should have been a turning point. Instead, world leaders continue to drag their feet, hesitant or unwilling to make far-reaching decisions that will prioritise the lives of their citizens in order to appease wealthy corporations and climate-change denialists. Things are only getting worse, not better, and we have very little time left to fix it. 'The window of opportunity for avoiding climate catastrophe is closing fast,' says Kofi Annan, former secretary-general of the United

Nations. 'The only promises that matter in Paris are those that are kept.'

For many who cannot comprehend the consequences of climate change, or refuse to acknowledge its existence, it is difficult to calculate the human cost of a small rise in the earth's temperature. But the link between climate change and human rights is observable, and the survival of one is wholly affected by the upsurge of the other. Rising oceans, prolonged droughts, tsunamis, flooding and extreme heatwaves will force millions of people to flee their homes, resulting in the proliferation of a new kind of refugee. And while it is currently people in developing nations suffering most as a result of global warning, in the long run, climate change has no favourites. Every single living being on this planet will feel the effects when our planet becomes too hot to sustain life.

It is imperative for citizens in all countries to evaluate their rights for addressing this issue, and to come together to create a lasting, workable solution to counter climate change. Those inflicting the most damage on the planet need to be held accountable for the harm they are doing to priceless natural resources and all the species who live on earth.

The Paris Agreement provides activists with some moral high ground. It is an acknowledgement by world leaders that change is needed. As concerned citizens, we have to ensure that our governments keep the promises they made in Paris to give up fossil fuels, to enforce carbon pricing on countries that emit the most greenhouse gases, and to provide the resources for creating renewable energy.

The Paris Agreement has legal power and should be ratified by parliaments in every country. Social movements, trade unions, political parties and progressive businesses must mobilise into action, to ensure that grand ambition is translated into concrete action. Subsidies for fossil fuels are estimated to cost $500 billion annually, but if only 30 per cent of those funds was invested in clean energy, emissions would drop by 18.15 per cent in the countries that were studied.[11]

The funds obtained from a carbon tax, a 'polluter pays' scheme, would facilitate a further move towards clean energy and renewable technology. According to a 2014 report from the World Bank, about forty countries and more than twenty cities, provinces and states have implemented some form of a carbon-pricing system into their environmental programmes.[12]

Cities in every country, with leaders who look to the future and not only the here and now, can drive an energy revolution. Transformation, tackling poverty, upward mobility, new industries and livelihoods – all of these require cheap electricity. Solar grid systems can be implemented in towns and suburbs until their use stimulates a 'roof revolution', enabling citizens to become their own energy producers while supplying the energy grid with their surplus. Such off-take agreements and appropriate investment in storage capacity will create a thriving solar industry that will lead to more jobs as well as address the large urban demand for energy.

In South Africa we have to start rethinking our energy mix as I believe Africa can be a front-runner in the race to a green future. The use of coal-fired power stations is in decline, and further moves are being made towards a renewable energy programme in the country, with more than forty-four facilities supplying 2.2 gigawatts of electricity.[13] Our government, however, continues to push for nuclear energy, claiming that it is the only viable solution for supplying most of South Africa with electricity. As a citizenship, we need to move away from conventional or outmoded ideas of energy production, and invest in strategies for meeting the energy needs of our growing and in many cases impoverished population.

This is not an impossible task. In the mid-nineties South Africa, still reeling from the effects of decades of racial segregation, faced an enormous challenge in providing the majority of its citizens with vital services that they were denied during apartheid. As minister of communications in Nelson Mandela's cabinet, my portfolio was tasked with finding the means of connecting our citizens technologically, as most did not have computers, access to the internet or even phones.

We decided to approach the issue from an African perspective, looking at it as something that had to be solved in an African way. It was our problem, and only when we knew where we wanted to go and had a plan, did we invite outside partners from other governments, international agencies such as the UN International Telecommunication Union, the private sector and civil society organisations to help us fully integrate our ideas.

In less than a decade we were able to leapfrog from having almost no infrastructure to providing many of our citizens with cutting-edge mobile technology, in the process creating one of the fastest-growing telecommunications markets in the world.

These technologies did not need any donor or government funding or seminars and workshops, and even impoverished citizens are now making efforts to participate in the global communications boom. The affordability and convenience of a prepaid card has given millions of Africans access to mobile communication technology, and today, mobile banking penetration is used by 12 per cent of sub-Saharan Africa's population, in comparison to 2 per cent globally.[14]

And yet despite these achievements, Africa is still experiencing a major energy crisis. It is estimated that over 600 000 Africans, nearly half of them children, die every year as a result of household air pollution caused by the use of charcoal and wood for cooking. Astronauts from space report seeing large pieces of the continent covered in darkness at night, while developed countries are bright halos of light. There is nothing stopping South Africans from applying the lessons learnt in our telecommunications venture to the development of an energy solution for the entire African continent.

With the right resources and a dynamic mobilisation of their citizens, African countries could revolutionise the global energy sector.

Our continent has an abundant supply of wind and solar resources, giving us the opportunity to bypass older, more destructive sources of energy such as fossil fuels. A report by the International Energy Agency claims that renewables could generate more than 40 per cent of all power capacity in Africa by 2040 through hydropower, wind and solar grid technology. This would not only reduce greenhouse emissions from industrialised countries such as South Africa and Nigeria, but also provide jobs to a number of citizens. If South Africa begins fervent campaigns to introduce widespread renewable energy to its citizens, by 2030 at least 73 000 people could be employed in the sector and hundreds of thousands of others in related sectors.[15]

This could be a game-changer for Africa, a continent that, when combined, has enough resources to become a world superpower. Perhaps this will be the catalyst for African countries to come together and create a continent-wide energy mix that makes maximum use of all the resources at our disposal and will increase our bargaining power in world politics. We have to stop purchasing old obsolete technology from overseas suppliers, all of which will become 'stranded assets' in the future, and inspire the brilliant minds that live here to invent new technology for Africa, by Africans. It is time to remove from our continent those forces that still see our territory as the dumping ground for their waste, our people and animals as the unfortunate casualties of their abuse of our resources. By seeking out new players who will work with us on building an industrial policy that places conservation, education and renewable energy before profits, we could easily steer our current technology into the twenty-first century.

It is time for Africans to start viewing our continent as one home and not just fifty-four separate countries. Our people have been the first to suffer the consequences of a rising earth temperature, and stand the risk of even greater suffering in the future. The growing refugee crisis, which has seen over sixty million people displaced from countries in Africa and Asia, continues to cause tensions in an already fraught global political climate. As more people are forced to escape floods, droughts and wars over resources because of global warming, we can expect an exacerbation of this issue – and this time it will not only be inhabitants of developing or war-torn nations fleeing their countries.

The world's environmental, humanitarian and developmental challenges have converged.

It is time for urgent action. *Trade unions, social organisations, students and ordinary citizens must be encouraged to fight for an ethical social and energy transition that embraces zero carbon, zero poverty and zero inequality paradigms.* Our stake in trillions of dollars' worth of pension funds is one way of leveraging investors to abandon fossil fuels for green technology.

The most essential change, however, has to be made to our behaviour, as we learn how to adapt to lower demands and adjusted economic trajectories that favour the use of renewables. There is never one 'silver bullet', so what we need are many small solutions that will together constitute a major leap forward.

We have no time to lose. There are millions of local community-building models that can collaborate and demand a new path of development.

14

The Right to Feel Human

SOME OF THE greatest lessons I have learnt in my life have been in the slums, in rural villages and on the factory floor. If only we – the educated, the literate, the more sophisticated second cousins of the middle class – could just learn to *listen* to the people who populate these areas.

When I visited Nairobi, Kenya, in mid-2014, I was reminded of the value of listening and the power it gives to the speaker when they realise their views are being heard and respected. In Mukuru Kwa Reuben slum, one of the largest in Nairobi, I sat and listened as women leaders spoke about the issues they faced every day.

These are people who live on the fringes of a ruptured society. Kenya might have won its independence over half a century ago, but many of its forty-four million inhabitants still live under the yokes of oppression and poverty. The sense of degradation this has brought them is not unlike what those suffering under colonial rule or apartheid felt – people who were denied basic rights and any idea that they were, in fact, human. 'I don't feel I am a Kenyan,' said Dorice, one of Mukuru Kwa Reuben's community leaders. 'I don't see anyone who respects us slum-dweller women. We are treated like dogs. We live in one room, with our children, even teenagers. We give birth there. We eat, sleep, cook and raise our children in these one-room shacks. We are forgotten.' I can almost feel her despair as she describes this life that she is forced to live.

Dorice and her teammates are part of a community self-help group that receives legal assistance and training courses from Akiba Mashinani, an innovative NGO that provides slum dwellers with housing assistance. Most are casual workers in the adjoining industrial district, an area that almost seems like a parallel universe to the one in which many of its labourers reside. Similar to township dwellers in South Africa, residents of Nairobi's slums live without electricity, running water and sanitation decades after democracy, while those in the cities are able to take full advantage of such services.

The faces of these women, worn and lined by years of hardship, reminded me of something else from home: the steely resolve that I frequently witnessed in workers from the labour movement as they learnt to fight in their own struggle for freedom. Before I visited Mukuru Kwa Reuben, I was warned of the dangers lurking in the crime-infested, filthy slum. But the strength that radiated from its leaders made me feel safe and nostalgic. I was among my kin, hardened warriors of social justice. For years I fought side by side with people just like them. And as we sat together under a lonely tree, shifting our chairs occasionally to avoid the heat of the sun, it felt like thirty years ago, when I visited South Africa's slums and villages and discussed building a union movement with hostel dwellers and community workers.

The fight that these Kenyan activists are waging might seem much smaller than a struggle for democracy, but it represents just how far away many Africans are from really achieving it. Although Kenya has the largest GDP in East and Central Africa, many of its citizens are still denied the most basic human rights, Dorice explained: 'We do not live the lives of middle-class women in the suburbs. Here we fight for the right to a toilet ... More often than not we use a basin in our shack and are forced to discard its contents into the open public drain. Life is hard.'

The right to a toilet is the political goal of slum-dwelling Kenyan activists. This is what citizens of a democratic country have to fight for.

Dorice took me to her house and described just how much this absence of adequate sanitation is harming her community. Besides the threat of disease, the lack of access to a personal toilet is dangerous for women, who risk being raped if they walk to the slum's public facilities at night. Thousands of girls also have to miss school when they have their periods because of the scarcity of public toilets in the area, or because they have no money to use them. It costs locals three shillings each time they use the public toilets. Dorice's activist group, which has collected over 5 000 signatures in a petition to the government about the issue, showed me just how broad a human rights problem not having a toilet really is.

The walk to Dorice's house was treacherous. We had to navigate rough, filthy pathways and open drains, and the stench of the sewage was unbearable. 'Infections, especially amongst our children, are a daily hazard,' she told me. 'You can see the disease in the water. These are impassable in the rains. They rise and flood our rooms, bringing havoc.'

The people I saw in the slum were clearly malnourished. Diseases such as malaria, typhoid, dysentery, tuberculosis and AIDS are commonplace.

When we arrived at Dorice's home, an informal two-roomed structure with corrugated-iron walls and a brick foundation, I felt saddened at the amount of effort she has put into keeping it presentable. It is minuscule; bunk beds, a table and a couch leaving one with hardly any space in which to move. But it is spotless, a reflection of Dorice's courage and fortitude. Living in a slum has not been enough to erode her sense of dignity.

Dorice shares this tiny space with her husband and two teenage children, which is another assault on her own and her family's self-esteem. 'There is no privacy,' she explained. 'When my husband wants to be intimate, it is so awkward.' She pointed to the fragile walls. 'When the rains come, we raise all the furniture. We pray that it stops. This is not the life I want my children to live.'

Contrary to what others might think of these slum dwellers, they know exactly what they do want.

Through the fundraising efforts of the women's self-help group, residents have been able to purchase twenty-three acres of land in the area and this will protect them from being forcefully evicted from their homes. In recent years, the growth in Nairobi's population has made formerly semi-urban territory like the slum lands more valuable, and the owners of this land, mostly companies and private individuals, are now desperate to remove the slum dwellers. Highly organised cartels with political connections operate in slum territory, and they use a brutal enforcement system to get votes out of slum residents or to evict them from their homes.

As in many countries with a history of colonialism, land is a highly politicised issue in Kenya. With more people leaving rural areas because of poverty and climate change, increased population pressure in the cities means land prices will continue to skyrocket. The abundance of labour in the slums, which border Nairobi's industrial parks, also adds to the value of slum land. But slum residents like Dorice and her fellow committee leaders have proven that they are more than cheap sources of labour. Their land-buying enterprise is exactly the kind of activism that needs to be utilised further in civil society. Initiative and action underline this kind of approach, rather than waiting around for handouts from donors or government.

Jane Weru, the executive director of Akiba Mashinani, explained how the organisation has worked with these women to help them find the tools that have brought them land independence. I found her calm yet enthusiastic outlook refreshing. 'We have just approved a new constitution and bill of rights,' she told me. 'It guarantees Kenyan citizens the right to sanitation, water, quality education and health. We have a right to a home. Yet we have had to fight a bitter struggle against forced removal. This land is now valuable and the cartels are now determined to profit by displacing families that have lived here for generations. We have just won a victory when the supreme court supported our right to stay. But we know that while we won that battle, the war is far from over.'

One of the war's battlegrounds is the slum's local school, attended by 491 pupils from Grades One to Eight. The headmistress, Winifred Maingi, showed me around the school building, which is nothing more than six classrooms that were built using donations from NGOs. I felt a knot forming in my stomach as I entered the first classroom. The scene was utterly tragic. The classroom floors are not tiled or carpeted, but hard and rough. They are all crudely partitioned. And there is no electricity, computers or libraries. Two toilets, holes in the ground, serve the entire school.

'Do you receive any help from government?' I asked some of the teachers.

They laughed. 'No,' they chorused. 'We have to pay ourselves ... We have to pay for everything.'

The school has twelve teachers and not much else because the community does not own the land on which the school is located and cannot receive a subsidy from the government as a result. Fees are 200 shillings a month, or two US dollars, which is a lot of money for parents. Many cannot afford to pay the twenty shillings a day for the school lunch of rice and beans and the children have to go without. A large number of children end up dropping out of school so that they can find work and help supplement the family income.

I asked the children in one classroom what they hope to be when they grow up. The hands shot up.

'An engineer to build houses,' one said. 'An aeronautical engineer,' said another. 'A social worker', 'a technician', 'a nurse', 'a teacher'.

They have dreams, some of them huge, and many reveal an awareness of their harsh reality and their sense of social responsibility. They hope to have careers that will improve service delivery and infrastructure in their communities rather than be famous or rich, as many children their age dream of becoming. Despite their need to do good, many will end up being victims of the same oppressive system as their parents, unless they are given a ladder out of their poverty.

During my walk through the slum, I was impressed by its thriving local economy. Vegetable sellers, hammer mills, makeshift clinics, water dispensers, privately owned toilets. Many of the people who run these micro ventures are women, the mothers of children at the local school.

A basic social grant will provide crucial support to these women, who will be able to put the extra funds towards their children's education.

This is a community that has had a few tastes of victory, and most have been achieved through the courage and perseverance displayed by its women leaders. By identifying themselves primarily with the roles that mean most to them – whether activists, mothers or entrepreneurs – these women have been able to determine which bread-and-butter issues they should attach the most importance to. When they commit to these issues, they do so with resilience, understanding that the struggle will be hard and long. They are a supreme example of the way the marginalised should organise, by focusing on the issues that hit them hardest, regardless of how small or inconsequential they might seem.

True activists must make sure that the voices of Dorice and so many other outstanding female community leaders are heard by those in power. We need to stop listening to the 'middlemen' in the global conversation about ending poverty, the supposed developmental activists who represent the interests of industries and corporations. During their stints in these areas they tend to organise a few workshops, introduce their plans for development that were drawn up with their Western donors, and then depart the second their budgets run out and they have ticked all their boxes. The area for which they had shown so much concern becomes nothing more than a dumping ground for their disparate projects, soon to be white elephants.

The next place I visited in Nairobi was Kibera, another gigantic informal settlement on the outskirts of the city.

Kennedy Odede is the founder of Shining Hope for Communities (SHOFCO), which provides basic, essential services to Kenyan slums, including clean water, sanitation, healthcare, education, electricity and roads. Odede told me what motivated him to begin working in community development: 'I am sick and tired of my family members dying of hunger and diarrhoea because we are so poor. In Kibera, people are desensitised to death. Living is the exception. We know we are invisible to the people who live in the suburbs of Nairobi and have jobs and nice houses. We should all have the right to live decent lives, have clinics with nurses, doctors and medicines, schools where our children can learn.'

Odede's passion to help his community was informed by his own childhood in a Kibera slum. The eldest of eight children in a family that had very few resources to go around, Odede said, 'I knew poverty and hunger before I learnt to walk or read.' By the time he was ten years old he was living on the streets.

Odede took me on a tour of the slum to show me some of the projects the Shining Hope had going. During the tour I was struck by the amount of respect showed to me by the locals. Before I arrived in the slum, I was warned that no one from 'the outside' ever goes into Kibera without security. But years in the union taught me that walking alongside community leaders and activists is often the best form of protection to have.

While we moved through the slum, Odede explained how he

went from being a street child to a community activist: 'I dreamt about changing my community. In 2004 I had a job in a factory earning $1 for ten hours of work. It was hard and dangerous labour. I walked hours to work because I could not afford the taxi fare. One day I came home from the job to see one of my good friends had been shot by the police. A week later, another hung himself in a tiny room. I couldn't take it any more. I took my savings of a few US dollars and bought a soccer ball and started Shining Hope for Communities.'

So how does a soccer ball change a community, I asked?

Odede enlightened me: 'We started with soccer and street theatre. My friends thought it was crazy – they said we needed a donor to start an NGO. I said, "This is not an NGO, this is a movement." I started to talk to the gangs. Through sport they became our strongest supporters. Our soccer team excelled. We won prizes. We started to have a big following. Residents were proud of us. And parents loved us because their children would be off the streets and away from drugs and criminal gangs.'

He led me to another SHOFCO initiative, the Marcus Garvey Library, where many of the 40 000 SHOFCO members have library cards. After stepping through a metal door, I found myself looking at a room with close to thirty people seated around several tables, all of them engrossed in books, magazines or papers. The place was silent. The librarian showed me her records: every one of the SHOFCO members has a smart card for which they pay a small fee, and this gives them access to a variety of services in the community, including the library. I was delighted to see how this innovative method of encouraging community involvement was also promoting reading and culture in the area.

All along the way to the next SHOFCO project we met entrepreneurs, shoemakers and airtime retailers who had received assistance from the organisation to set up their own businesses through a SHOFCO micro-credit system. SHOFCO's ethical loan practices have helped to push out unscrupulous moneylenders and hostile loan sharks from the community.

Our next stop was a clinic for lactating and pregnant mothers which reminded me of the Mothers' Club in Bangladesh. Parents present their SHOFCO smart cards at the clinic, which helps the staff keep a record of all visits. At the clinic babies can be weighed and immunised, and mothers receive advice on breastfeeding and HIV/AIDS.

They even have their own blood-testing laboratory on site. The level of detail in these projects impressed me and I asked Odede where he got all his genius ideas from.

'I was lucky,' he replied. 'I was noticed and offered a scholarship at Wesleyan University [in Connecticut, USA]. I graduated but came straight back to Kibera. This is my home. I wanted to plough back into my community hope and opportunity.'

After my tour of the slum I met up with a group of young SHOFCO workers and volunteers for a traditional lunch of *skumawiki* (a green leaf similar to kale) and *ugali* (maize bread) with chicken stew. It was delicious. When I asked about the challenges that Kenya faced, I was not surprised to find out that they stemmed from the same problem that people all over the world experience: inequality.

'Our biggest worry is tribalism,' one of them told me. 'It is the weapon of the predatory elites. They use the poor to fight their battles. They throw pennies to us and become rich by dividing us. A poor person is too busy scrounging income to put food on the table every day.' His words sparked a heated debate. Would the recent discovery of oil in Turkana in the north of Kenya cause more ethnic and resource conflicts or would it be the start of inclusive growth in the region?

Throughout our discussion, I could sense the pride and potential in each of the young activists. They are not going to accept the ongoing corruption and mediocre leaders who keep Africans poor even with all the gold, diamonds and platinum resting right under our feet. They represent the future of the activist movement in Africa and the interests of its growing youth population, which is steadily on the rise. Currently half of the billion people on our continent are under twenty years old, and by 2050, when the African population doubles, 70 per cent will be under twenty-five.[1]

That is a lot of incredible human energy.

I met a group of future activists when I visited a school in the Kibera region. During their history lessons they learnt about Steve Biko and Martin Luther King, and were wide-eyed when I told them I had heard the former speak when I was fifteen and had worked with the great Nelson Mandela.

Their awe when hearing about my encounters with two of Africa's greatest freedom fighters was a heart-warming and gratifying sight. Through SHOFCO's educational programme, these impressionable young minds were being taught about African leaders and how they had used knowledge and idealism to inspire millions of people into taking action. These children were discovering appropriate role models, icons they could relate to, not criminals or gangsters. 'We must capture the potential of urban youth before they are led to believe that the path of violence is their only option,' Odede emphasised. 'Instead of investing billions of dollars on drones and arms for the police and military, let's focus on creating economic opportunities for our youth and providing basic and essential services like healthcare and education.'

Shining Hope's prioritising of education is what drives the organisation's innovation and entrepreneurial energy, and what has made it the largest developmental organisation in Nairobi. To me, these people are the real leaders of Africa. They have sourced and created everything they need, even though they do not have a government that values them as citizens. They are changing their world, one step at a time, one person at a time. This is a war that is worth fighting, Odede told me.

'Everything is political,' he said. 'We need to self-organise. We need to free our minds. We need to unite our communities. We need to create our own livelihoods.'

Our challenge as activists is how to turn that into our global reality.

15

The Naledi Star

I N BUSINESS JARGON there is something known as a 'put up or shut up' clause. It is the point during a merger when real money has to change hands or the whole deal unravels.

After reaching the summit of Kilimanjaro and seeing the splendour of the African landscape laid out before me, I realised I had reached my own 'put up or shut up' point. I had to either do something to help fix what was wrong with the current system, or go on with my life and stop whining about bad governments and predatory elites.

At the end of 2013, a year before I set out on my Kilimanjaro adventure, I joined up with two of my comrades, Gino Govender and Kumi Naidoo, and we had a long reflective discussion about our hopes for the future of South Africa and the rest of the world. During apartheid we had worked together as community activists in Durban's Indian townships, and I know how much they care about this country. Kumi has been a social justice campaigner for most of his life, was the head of Greenpeace International for six years, and is currently the director of Africans Rising, a pan-African civil society movement. Gino was a prominent figure in South African unions and has worked for the National Union of Mineworkers (NUM) and COSATU, as well as globally in the mining and chemical union movements.

During our discussion we tried to put our individual experiences in a larger context, looking at them in relation to South Africa and the global village. The lessons we learnt as activists still resonated with us, and like many others, we wanted to return to our roots and work with the people again as we used to, co-creating futures with local communities.

By this time we were experienced enough to know that things are never that simple. It has been over a quarter of a century since Nelson Mandela completed his long walk to freedom, and the country he went on to lead is still in a tenuous state, full of complex politics, conflict and history that frequently generates discord. The current state of our government may have been unforeseeable to its citizens at the dawn of democracy, but even then the cracks created by factionalism and political prejudices were starting to show in public. The fight against apartheid, and the battles that subsequently followed it, were never simply black and white, or about black against white. Mandela may have dumped his oppressive prison garb for colourful silk shirts, singing his melody of unity and reconciliation, but that was the furthest he could go. He was a symbol of the 'free man', and yet there were fewer men less free than him. His responsibilities made him a constant prisoner, his jail cell this time being one of conscience and struggle. As the founding father of our democracy, he should be seen above all as a symbol of human endurance.

If Mandela's example has taught us anything, it is that freedom is not an automatic privilege. It makes continuous demands, and demands continuous vigilance. It means becoming custodians of our own lives and rejecting the notion that another Mandela will come along to save us. It forces us to make proper historical assessments of Mandela himself – no beatifications, canonisations or shrines. We should preserve his memory, but more importantly we need to act on it.

We can begin by acknowledging that despite the massive achievements of Mandela's government, we still made many mistakes during our transition. The dissolution of the apartheid regime could not be acquired without the metaphorical pound of neoliberal flesh. In South Africa's desire to be a player in global capitalism, we seem to have adopted the tenets of the former regime's philosophy of power, greed and elitism.

Instead of utilising our resources for our own people, we took to selling them to the wealthiest buyer. Today, so much of this country's land lies idle, used only for weekend excursions by absentee landlords. The number of productive farmers is declining rapidly. Even around rural towns, huge shanty towns mushroom, the result of farmworkers being evicted or leaving farms that are abandoned. After democracy, South Africa's neglected or unused land should have been shared with black farmworkers. They could have learnt about the industry from white farmers and become entrepreneurs too, benefiting from and adding value to the local food chain.

The first government of our early democracy could have fostered greater social cohesion through this strategy, literally by starting from the ground up. Perhaps if we had negotiated with potential and former stakeholders of South African land and asked them to work together for a more prosperous society, we could have learnt to shed some of the prejudices that still exist between us. By seeing ourselves as equal citizens with similar prerogatives, we would have had no option but to compromise. The mythology of the 'rainbow nation' should never have been imposed from the top, but built painstakingly from the messiness and disarray from below.

Today millions of South Africans could have had community-driven livelihoods through agriculture, as well as household food security, which would have eliminated malnutrition and reduced poverty enormously as the Stop Hunger campaign did in Brazil. Local governments could have set up commodity exchanges and marketplaces for rural farmers, insisting that all public institutions, such as schools, public hospitals and correctional facilities, obtain a third of their produce from family- and community-farming schemes. With access to a state-guaranteed credit market as well as extension services, South Africa might have had a thriving farming community providing a livelihood to millions of our citizens.

It is not too late to put this initiative into effect right now and end the monopolisation of South Africa's wealth by an old white establishment that continues to exclude the black majority. The disparity in wealth is so large that three individuals have as much wealth as half of the population, or about 28 million citizens. Twenty-two years after apartheid, inequality has actually increased, with unemployment at a record high and one in four South Africans going hungry every day with little chance of getting any food.[1]

The newly established democratic government did not change the structure of the previous regime's economy. After the demise of the Reconstruction and Development Programme, a new class of the super-rich was born. Big capital advanced a 'don't rock the boat' agenda, its prophets ensuring that nothing interfered in the management of their large corporations. To keep the wealth they had plundered safe, our government gave them permission to take it overseas and legally disinvest from South Africa. A policy of black economic empowerment was promoted which made a small number of people spectacularly wealthy rather than lifting a large number out of poverty. Meanwhile, the huge black underclass continued to grow and its access to wealth and land remained minuscule.

During my tenure as minister without portfolio in Mandela's government, it was my job to reconcile the aims of the 1955 Freedom Charter – which demanded the restoration of land to all citizens – with the developmental aims of the RDP. But there were those in the GNU, already sold on a neoliberal agenda, who believed the egalitarian approach to be a pipe-dream. Their argument was that disrupting prevailing economic orthodoxy would cause economic chaos, and that the new South Africa rather had to find ways of adapting to it. So we adapted and became 'normal', our remarkable, landmark negotiation for democracy in 1994 undermined by the same practices that strengthened the corrupt apartheid regime and those who had amassed fortunes by collaborating with it.

Following my journey up Kilimanjaro in 2014, twenty years after the breakdown of the RDP, I decided it was time to go back to the drawing board. With my comrades Naidoo and Govender, I returned to my roots as a community organiser and began a non-profit enterprise called EarthRise Trust, which sets out to cultivate South Africa's greatest resource, its land, for its people. To begin with, we purchased a 273-hectare parcel of territory in the east of the Free State next to the Lesotho border.

The area where we began working was Rustler's Valley, home to the local Naledi village. It was a small place to start, yes, but having not been able to help solve South Africa's political problems while in government, I could now do something small for impoverished communities in my own backyard. Years of union campaigning and lessons from some of the developing world's most impoverished societies had taught me that this is often the best place to start. Perhaps I would even go one step further and turn this project into a model of self-sustainability that could be scaled up in other communities. I have witnessed many times how progress begins with just a few people working conscientiously to achieve small local goals.

The long history of Rustler's Valley also attached some significance and sense of redress to EarthRise's objective of returning land to the people. In the nineteenth century, the valley was a favourite spot for white South African farmers, who travelled regularly to the area to seize cattle from Basotho people, and vice versa.

But Rustler's Valley's history goes back even further than that, to tens of thousands of years ago when San tribes inhabited its mountains and caves. In the 1800s, some of the Sotho fled to the valley to escape the war with the Zulus, journeying over the Maluti Mountains to found the kingdom of Lesotho. Around the same period, Afrikaners were also passing through the valley during their Great Trek between 1835 and 1846.

So much history, and much of it unknown or overlooked. By the 1980s the area was hosting the 'anti-establishment' parties of tourists, hippies, hipsters and electronic-music aficionados from around the world, until the lodge and other buildings were destroyed in a fire in 2007. It is the South African condition for stories to remain disparate and unreconciled, and this recent iteration of Rustler's Valley as a cheerful hangout location for young privileged individuals makes it easy to forget that it was, and continues to be, the site of numerous injustices against black people.

The residents of Naledi village, currently home to approximately 170 people, have been in the area for many generations and are familiar with and an important part of its past. Some of the men from Naledi – which means 'star' in Sesotho – as well as men from the neighbouring Franshoek village, worked at the mines during apartheid. Like other migrant labourers, they had to get permission from the owners of the land on which they lived to leave the farms, and were often forced to do a month of 'free' labour in payment for this 'favour'. In most cases the children of black farmers were pulled out of school to work on the farms during harvests, and were then compelled to leave the property when they turned eighteen. While capitalism has replaced feudalism and slavery in modern Western society, in many parts of rural South Africa this mode of production still exists in order to keep black inhabitants impoverished.

But despite the desperation of their circumstances, the residents of Naledi are committed to improving their lives and those of their children. When EarthRise began its work in the village, however, they were still not owners of the land on which they had lived and worked for many years, making them vulnerable at any time to eviction by the farmer who owned it. A few years before EarthRise came to the village, families on a neighbouring farm had been evicted and resettled in Franshoek because the farmer no longer wanted them living there. Millions of South Africans in rural areas have to live in this state of constant insecurity, subject to the mercy of both white landlords and traditional tribal authorities who control communally owned land that was part of the former Bantustans. Some of the largest land grabs in South Africa have been initiated by government to consolidate power in the hands of traditional chiefs rather than to offer them stewardship roles, which had been the policy of the new democratic government when it came to power in 1994. A number of these leaders have entered into deals with mining and agricultural companies eager to use the land for its natural and mineral resources. As a result, entire communities that have lived on the land for generations have been displaced.

The rural communities who have been living on this land for many years, sometimes decades, are not given the chance to address or oppose such developments. They do not have access to legal representation and are usually not consulted on any process of land transferral between traditional chiefs holding it in stewardship and the corporations taking it over.

In Rustler's Valley, however, the land had always been owned by white farmers. It was EarthRise's aim to remove the constraints that left black people on these farms vulnerable to eviction, and to offer them enough independence to begin creating their own wealth. Borrowing ideas from the work we had done as political activists, we as EarthRise's founders sat down to discuss our plans with Naledi residents and to work out how we could facilitate an agreed-upon solution for the future.

During our discussions we focused on a few key questions. What problem were we trying to solve? Whose problem was it? How were we going to solve it? And who was going to solve it?

We listened carefully as the community shared their hopes and concerns with us. This took many months, but it was crucial if EarthRise hoped to effect any real change in the community.

For me, these discussions were important in understanding what had changed for communities such as Naledi in twenty-two years of democracy. Despite obtaining 'freedom' with the fall of apartheid, Naledi, like thousands of other villages, was still without land tenure rights, running water, electricity or sanitation. Democracy was clearly not working here. The village school was dilapidated and lacking in resources, causing the children to while away their time by watching cars passing the village during the day. Fifteen years into the twenty-first century and Naledi residents were still living in an old-fashioned feudal system that gave all power and wealth to a white employer.

We had to change the context in which this inequality occurred, but only by working with the community to create a new system that would bring them communal wealth. This entailed questioning everyone who had a stake in the community's development and who hoped to guide it to a new future. We had to determine what kind of leaders would do this and not misuse the community's wealth for their own ends.

This was one of the main reasons for Naledi's willingness to work with EarthRise. They had feared that a commercial farmer would buy the land and serve them with another string of eviction notices. At the same time EarthRise was happy to be working with a community that wanted to take an active role in its development. They knew us by reputation, and believed we would give many of them jobs.

But there was the problem. EarthRise did not have money to employ Naledi's residents. So we decided that the best way to work with the village would be to follow a model that created employment and autonomy within the community, not outside it. To do this, we began a formal partnership with Naledi, devising a strategy for its growth through shared ideas and the pooling of resources.

The farm would become a non-profit trust and we as owners gave a portion of it to the community, using the rest for a shared enterprise that would enable growth through community-driven livelihoods in agriculture and various other village enterprises. The model we followed emphasised the creation of socially useful work that would deliver valuable goods and services to the people of the village.

EarthRise transferred forty-two hectares of arable land directly to the community at no cost. Once they were citizens of an independent village, they would never again have to face the prospect of eviction. This gave them scope to start imagining a new reality in which they could construct their own homes on their own land. Our shared vision was to build a beautiful community by working with its people, and ultimately creating pathways of hope and opportunity for the children who make up a third of the village.

There were, however, certain obstacles getting in the way of reaching this future. The administrative process of land transfer was bureaucratic and costly. The Naledi Village Committee wrote a letter to the government requesting legal assistance and EarthRise supported them in their negotiations with government officials. The local ward councillor, following discussions with the village committee, supported the application and the land was demarcated by the land surveyor's office before being registered by the name Naledi Village Development Trust.

The village then requested help from the councillor on another critical matter. A neighbouring white farmer had cut off Naledi's water supply because he believed someone in the village had stolen something from him. This sort of all-encompassing punishment by farm owners is common and also illegal, as all mineral and natural resources are held in trust by the state. After the community raised the matter with their municipality, they received water from a tanker sent to the village twice a week. But Naledi was right to insist on a long-term solution that would not have it dependent on a supply of water that would eventually come to an end. They requested that the municipality either force the farmer to comply with the law and restore the water supply, or arrange for a borehole to be drilled in the village.

The municipality chose the second option, sending in a team to drill a borehole, but without consulting the community on its specifications or where it should be located. For water to be pumped up from the hole, a diesel generator had to be acquired, and there was no agreement on who would pay for the diesel. These discussions did not take place mainly because the municipal official in charge of the process was never available on site.

Eventually a provincial government team ruled that the whole project had been mismanaged. The borehole was situated too close to the village cemetery and there was no guarantee that it was safe to drink. A hydrological survey found a water source further up the farm, and a plan was devised to use gravity to feed water to the tanks and distribute it to homes in the village. But the plan was never implemented. Two years have passed since the survey and the issue remains unresolved. When another drilling operation was undertaken, the village leaders were again not consulted and a hole was drilled in the wrong place. The drilling team left soon afterwards and the village remains without water.

This was Araku all over again. And while maladministration and corruption at a national level always dominate the news headlines, the worst hit by these incidents are often voiceless people in townships and villages under municipal government. Local government corruption and mismanagement rarely make the headlines like Nkandla or an arms or nuclear deal do, but they have a devastating impact on the lives of impoverished rural residents. For a long time they resign themselves to being subservient to arrogant state officials and accept the crumbs they receive from social grants and food parcels. But soon enough their anger explodes and violence ensues. When calm eventually returns, it is only temporary, the pent-up rage of residents often turning into a morass of hopelessness until the next explosion takes place.

Through our work in Naledi village, EarthRise sought to alleviate some of the community's frustration by helping them create a sustainable income of their own. To progress, the village had to remove itself from the classist, racist drama of twenty-first-century South African politics and focus on matters that directly affected its circumstances.

For the reconstruction of the farm, we agreed on a construction plan for many buildings which had burnt down, and the restoration of water and electricity supplies which had been disconnected some years previously. Turning to the village elders for their advice on which structures should take priority, it was decided that an old lodge near the farm should be renovated into an eco-lodge and conference centre that would help fund the farm and village development. A comprehensive skills-building programme in brick-laying, landscaping and electric work would drive the construction phase, but first we decided to determine what skills people in the village already possessed.

The results were not surprising to us. In the village and in neighbouring communities were men and women with a wide base of skills in construction. Many had acquired these skills during apartheid when the hated migrant system provided cheap labour to the mining and industrial sectors, as well as to neighbouring farmers.

Those with building, maintenance and landscaping skills were integral for the renovation of the lodge, and were divided into teams in which they could best utilise their experience. They would be important contributors to the redesign of their village into a twenty-first-century development.

Before we jumped head on into the renovation phase, the construction crew and those of us from EarthRise sat together and discussed how the village residents could participate both individually and collectively in rebuilding the farm. During the conversation, EarthRise emphasised that there should not be 'workers' creating the vision, but rather people building their future. We did not want a return to the old system of workers and bosses.

We also agreed on minimum wage rates – almost two-and-half

times what their counterparts were getting on other farms and for a forty-hour work week. We spoke about owning the work, respecting the labour of others, and about working safely.

The process was painstaking. Months were spent debating how we would work together, what all our rights and responsibilities were, and how to increase community involvement and ownership as we went forward. There were interpreters at every meeting so that no one was ever excluded from the conversation. Every member of the community was asked to spell out their aspirations and future career paths. The idea was to arrive at a point where community achievements could be supplemented with individual success.

I found the experience exhilarating. It was great to be organising at grassroots again! We dealt in none of the absurd politics of NGOs that had previously tried to 'fix' Naledi before giving up very quickly. One NGO had even raised money for Naledi from the national lottery and promptly disappeared with the cash. This kind of corruption is not unusual in the development industry.

The EarthRise Mountain Lodge was officially opened on 1 May 2015 with Jappie Lephatsi, who was born in Franshoek, employed as the lodge manager. The rest of the lodge's staff all came from the village. The profits from this social enterprise currently support development projects in the village and on the Naledi farm.

Jappie's story is an inspirational one. Throughout his life he has shown incredible strength in the face of horrifying abuses of spirit and body. The suffering started early, during his childhood, when he and his family, along with all their black neighbours, were evicted from the Franshoek farm in 1986 and moved into one village. Jappie recalled the restrictive and hostile atmosphere of his new home during that time, as black residents were not allowed to do anything that might upset their landlords. 'In those days it was difficult to even walk on the mountains, to see the birds and other animals,' he said. 'But we broke the law because we were curious. And we were thrashed. Sometimes twice, even by our parents, who feared being thrown off the farm.'

When Jappie was nineteen he was desperate to leave this world behind, where 'the law' forbade him from even taking a stroll near his home. 'There had to be something better in the world outside the farm,' Jappie thought. 'I applied to work on the mines. I heard that they needed workers at President Steyn, one of the largest gold mines in the world, situated at Welkom in the Free State about two hours away.' But to get the job, Jappie had to get permission from the farmer on whose land he lived, who promised to give his written consent only if Jappie worked for him for two months without pay. Determined to go, Jappie said he 'had no choice' but to accept the farmer's offer. 'But I got the job and looked forward to leaving,' he added.

But when Jappie arrived at the mines and saw what kind of conditions he would be living in, he realised that he had just traded one prison for another.

'The mines were not better,' he realised. 'It was harsh and brutal, like a jail. We slept in dormitories, sixteen per room. They housed thousands of workers. Nothing was private. When we went to the toilet it was a row of holes in a long line. It humiliated me every time as a youngster sitting with older people who I was always taught to respect.

'If we broke the rules, found with a knife or [were] absent [from work], it was straight to the jail for us. There, white farmers would take us and we would be forced to work on their farms. When we ate, the pap was dished with a spade and the gravy was bones and cartilage. There was a requirement every month for a big injection before you got paid. There was no explanation. We were told to just stand in a line.'

Eventually, however, conditions began changing for the mineworkers when the unions gained more power.

'We saw people discussing in small groups,' Jappie recalled with a smile. 'After a while I was invited. The union was coming. It was the National Union of Mineworkers. There were big fights as the management found out. Activists disappeared, summarily dismissed. But then the majority decided they wanted the union. The mine bosses were forced to recognise the union. Our lives started to change. The food improved. The injections stopped. Our wages and working conditions improved.'

He laughs. 'Jay, we stopped being treated like animals. The big federation, COSATU, was launched in December 1985 … We celebrated. The whites were angry and wanted to smash us. But we were too strong: "An injury to one is an injury to all" was the slogan COSATU taught us.'

When the union movement rallied black workers around the same cause of improved worker conditions, Jappie says that the white establishment 'started to respect us'. A turning point came when the *indunas*, or headmen, virtual prison guards at the hostels, were replaced with elected representatives of the miners known as 'senators'. After this, living relations at the hostels became more democratic.

Following a strike by the miners in 1987, the longest and biggest strike in South Africa at that stage, Jappie was certain that 'freedom was coming' to the country. The strike, led by the NUM, the second-largest union in the country, brought together 360 000 mineworkers to protest their wages and living conditions. It lasted three weeks, cost the mines hundreds of millions of rands and caused widespread chaos, with eleven people dead and 400 in jail. If any event was a sure sign that black South Africans would no longer tolerate racial oppression, it was this.

The mines fired 50 000 workers in an attempt to end the strike, but it did nothing to quell the workers' anger. Jappie remembers that at 'President Steyn, a stronghold of the union, thousands of workers were fired. But we were not defeated. We now knew how to fight. Never again would they keep us down. We went back and started to reorganise. Our time would come.'

And so it did. Two years after the NUM strike, the Mass Democratic Movement led by the UDF and COSATU launched its defiance
campaign, in which thousands of black citizens violated apartheid laws that kept them from using facilities or visiting areas that
were preserved for whites. What was at first a storm of protest
became a virtual hurricane. We soon managed to break the system,
and Nelson Mandela, the symbol of our victory, was released from
prison on 11 February 1990. Jappie's face lit up when he remembered
this moment.

'When Tata Madiba walked out of Victor Verster, we knew we
were within reach of our goal. We would be free. And so it happened. I went to vote on 27 April in 1994. When I entered the voting
booth, I felt the joy of my ancestors as I placed my cross next to
the face of Tata Madiba. I knew as a member of the NUM we
had made a great contribution to win our freedom.'

It would be another twelve years before Jappie returned to his
childhood home on Franshoek farm. The President Steyn mine
closed down in 2006 and Jappie was offered a position at another
mine, but he declined. 'I wanted to go back to my family,' he
explained. 'The NUM negotiated comprehensive training that
reskilled workers who were retrenched for life after the mines. I did
an electrical course. I went back to the farm, knowing I had a livelihood. I started to raise pigs and grow fruit trees. My wife Elsie
knew how to make jams. We were earning a decent living and able
to make sure our children got a good education. But then the
farmer demanded that we get rid of our pigs and cut down the fruit
trees. I had to get another job. I went to work in the lodge.'

Jappie showed no bitterness about experiencing yet another
form of discrimination from a white farmer. Years of struggle against
racism have made him resilient, resourceful and unselfish. As the
proud manager of the EarthRise Mountain Lodge, he shows incredible generosity even to those who have been cruel to him in the
past. It is hard to get rid of the constant smile on his face and his

unshakeable good humour, and he revels in sharing his skills. All electrical work at the lodge has been done by Jappie, and he has taught other members of the community these skills as well. The team under him all have job descriptions which are in compliance with the wage determination for the area, and they each have contracts for work in Rustler's Valley.

These occurrences have sparked huge discussion in other villages in the region and around the valley. Communities wanted to know why they could not have the same opportunities as their neighbours in Naledi. Soon general wages in accordance with labour standards in the district became common. And unlike many other parts of the country where people had to strike, use force or engage in formalised negotiations to achieve these goals, none of this happened in Rustler's Valley.

The EarthRise movement in Naledi has become a spark that could one day lead to an explosion in all of South Africa's rural communities. Our work in one tiny village has started a conversation in many villages in the district, and even in other parts of the country. But we also knew when we began our project that there were still many struggles ahead. And the next phase of development, which was to lift Naledi residents out of poverty, would be much more difficult to achieve. It was time to create a sustainable local economy for Naledi based on agricultural and social enterprises. Whether this would work in a country with an economic system that promotes inequality and elitism, and which has its tentacles even in the isolated village of Naledi, was another matter.

16

Real Change

THE CRUCIAL ROLE of money in most social interactions has always made a great impression on me. Just like many people around the world, I have experienced the degradation and anxiety of those who have little of it, as well as resentment and anger at those who have too much of it. This kind of socio-economic system works at keeping these two groups apart only insofar as allowing the privileged to keep accumulating wealth at the expense of the poor.

In 1958, when I was four years old, my family was evicted from my childhood home under apartheid's Group Areas Act. This naturally affected my own and my parents' sense of self-worth, and it might have been the reason for my father's decision not to have us move to the dormitory townships that were set up exclusively for Durban Indians. Instead, he bought a piece of land in a developing area on the outskirts of the city called Reservoir Hills.

Very few houses had been built in the area at this point, and there was barely any infrastructure to serve the community either. As Reservoir Hills became more developed and received roads and electricity, an image of bare-chested black workers digging the trenches, singing a soulful Zulu rhyme of hardship, remains entrenched in my mind. What stood out most about these scenes was the ever-present white supervisor who sat and watched as the labourers being paid a pittance performed back-breaking work.

I felt deeply angered by this, and not just about the blatant racism of it all. I experienced the same rage whenever a wealthy family moved into the larger houses in my neighbourhood and drove around in their fancy cars. Many of them were snobbish and condescending, choosing to shield themselves from their poorer neighbours by hiding away in their bubbles of privilege.

I became fascinated with why some people had money and others could barely feed their families. If we are all apparently born equal, then why is the way we live our lives not equal too?

I came to realise that at some point between the two milestones of birth and death, certain events occur that determine what your place will be in this world and whether you will share in the privilege of the wealthy or the misery of the poor. In apartheid (and present-day) South Africa, skin colour was a key driver in determining which group you fell into. The apartheid premise for wealth distribution was unconditional in who was qualified to have it, and the government was militant in ensuring that those who were unqualified rarely came close to receiving it.

But none of this provided a sufficient explanation for wealth inequalities that existed in black communities like my own.

I found an answer for this when I realised that people who were born to households with more wealth tended to 'succeed' more easily than those from poor backgrounds. The workers I saw toiling on the road were doing all the hard work but they would remain poor, and die that way, while their white bosses took the credit for their work as well as most of the money. The latter's children thereby had an easier path to success and wealth, while the children of black labourers were most likely to follow in their parents' footsteps, leaving school early or not attending school at all so as to find work. I had witnessed this in my own circle of family and friends, many of whom worked hard but still struggled to make a living.

People with careers that involved caring for or mentoring entire communities or large groups of children, such as priests, teachers and nurses, were rarely the beneficiaries of the wealth that upheld a powerful capitalist system.

But this is what capitalism does. Community workers are in the wrong business if they hope to become rich through their efforts. Property, not people, forms the basis of capitalist philosophy. Within this framework people are divided into two distinct classes: the means of production and the wealthy owners of property. Those without wealth have only their labour with which to earn a livelihood, while those with wealth have the resources to buy property, which will bring them more wealth. Workers, who constitute a critical aspect of production, are largely excluded from deciding what is produced, how and where it is produced, and in what way output of production achieves value in markets. Once products have realised their worth, workers are also excluded from determining the use of surpluses, including profits, and how these are distributed.

In contrast, those who own goods and property have a say in every aspect of their production. And they can increase and maintain the wealth they have made in this process by participating in it for as long as they have capital, as well as by transferring it to their families. This is one of the ways in which capitalism infiltrates every level of society, prescribing types of social organisation such as the structure of families and households, or who is entitled to get what from whom. These decisions have influenced our beliefs and viewpoints, including those of patriarchy and religion, and made it possible for such a system to be reproduced successfully in numerous cultures around the world. Out of all the species that exist on the planet, it is only humans who use a proxy for value – money – to arbitrate social relationships, facilitate our well-being, and inform our definitions of how we live on earth.

Capitalism is the explanation for widespread inequality and the reason that wealth for some and poverty for many others is perceived as a natural way of being.

This is patently a false premise. There is no inherent fault or flaw in any person that predisposes or justifies their living in poverty. In my lifetime I have seen countless struggles by individuals and groups against inequality, and there is no reason for subjecting so many people to such an unjust order of being.

While capitalism superseded the old feudal system that favoured hereditary nobility, its dissection of the planet into commodified private properties does not constitute the end of history. Instead, as the contemporary capitalist crisis intensifies and its effects are felt globally, we have begun to observe the emergence of a socio-economic and political system that is ostensibly post-capitalist. This new economic atmosphere is dominated by self-sustaining communities that embrace participation, sufficiently remunerate those who provide it with useful services and pay proper respect to the environment. Naledi village, alongside millions of such local economies, is the testing ground for this new system of living and interacting.

When EarthRise began organising in Naledi, there were numerous factors to take into account before we got started, including an idea of where to start. We knew we had to create jobs, but we had to figure out how they would be remunerated.

Again, there were vital gains to be made from the kind of cooperative movement espoused by activist organisations such as trade unions. The same underlying principle determines every manifestation of the genuine union movement, and that is *solidarity*.

The selfishness and materialism underlining the capitalist approach to people and planet are not only useless from a social or communal point of view, but completely distasteful from a humane or charitable perspective as well. Instead of enclosing our minds around ideas of individualism and self-importance, we could come together as communities, searching for our strength and wealth in one another.

In the village of Naledi, strength and wealth could be found in a number of things that so many of us take for granted – sanitation, houses, clean water and food. But for a very long time it seemed as if these basic rights were only the privilege of people who lived far away in cities and suburbs.

With the support of EarthRise Trust, these villagers were given a choice. They did not have to wait for social grants or donations to access basic goods and services. They did not have to live in or near a city either. Why go to a store and buy food when they could grow it themselves? In fact, they could even open their own store and sell or exchange whatever produce exceeded their needs. Instead of depending on an economy that serves the needs of a few rich individuals, Naledi could build a local economy that counts on the input and welfare of every individual – in essence, an economy that profits an entire community of individuals.

Of course, there are risks to such a plan. Naledi has hosted several cooperatives in its past, both local and international, and many were discredited when they proved to be more about corporates than about cooperating, sometimes indistinguishable from businesses owned by private shareholders. In other cases cooperatives had shown up in Naledi and failed, functioning only as decoys for government leaders, who in their supposed concern for the community had failed to include it in the implementation of their initiatives.

Nonetheless, EarthRise still believed that a sustainable cooperative would be a good thing for Naledi. We just had to ensure that the Rustler's Valley Naledi Farmers Co-op worked for the community by fulfilling realistic goals and producing useful goods that would sustain its needs. We required entrepreneurs who could work around a shared-services model that ensured every co-op member put their fair share of work into the organisation. This was the way COSATU was run in the eighties, with every member playing their part in the

union's development. It is what made the union so great at mobilising an entire community against apartheid injustices.

In Naledi the first crops were planted during a prolonged drought
that affected the region in 2015 and 2016. Members chose not to
wait for it to end given the reality of climate change, which makes it
difficult to predict what the weather will do next. If the community succeeded under this worst-case scenario, it would also break
any psychological barriers preventing residents from believing they
could progress in this venture.

EarthRise Trust invested a small amount of money into the co-op
to help get it started. We approached other partners to support
the village as well, managing to sign on the Old Mutual Foundation
and an NGO called Afrigrow, which provided the seed capital and
technical training that the co-op needed.

Within six months the co-op was growing thousands of kilo-
grams of tomatoes, cabbage, spinach and pumpkins. The villagers
could not believe it. They had enough food to feed their families
and supply the village school, as well as other schools in the district,
with food. The story of Rustler's Valley began to change. It was no
longer just a secluded spot for hippies or the location of an impoverished village, but a community that was developing through shared
input and profit. It became a model of a self-sustaining village for
other community initiatives as well, and an important source of
food for neighbouring villages. Soon trucks and bakkies from towns
from as far away as Lesotho were coming to Naledi to purchase produce, in the process strengthening the economic situation of the
village and improving the lives of its residents.

The villagers began working on other projects for increasing their
productivity and attracting tourists to the region. A Dutch charity
called Zorg van de Zaak, which advances community-driven initiatives, provided Naledi with a small donation for its 'incubator fund'
for micro-enterprises. Many workshops later, and the projects identified as a priority for the region were poultry/egg production, a

nursery for vegetable seedlings, a bakery, a mountain-bike club and a creative venture promoting indigenous music, local crafts, music and art. The social organisation that was envisioned emphasised the value of production for communities, unlike the co-ops that functioned in apartheid South Africa which were set up by white farmers to capture surplus value for themselves at the expense of the local population.

A third leg of the community development programme is a 'Working for Water' project that aims to clear alien or foreign vegetation from the valley that depletes its water supply. I had been involved in such projects with the RDP in the mid-nineties, and I knew how advantageous such an initiative could be for a community. It teaches villagers various skills, such as first-aid and how to use heavy machinery; creates jobs for those involved in the project; and helps establish small enterprises for using wood off-cuts.

In 2015 the Naledi Village Committee applied to the local government for their sponsorship of the programme and a partnership was established. Twenty members of the community were recruited for training in forestry management. However, since 2016 the project has been suspended because of local political conflicts, and the community's water supply is still restricted. Even in this rural microcosm, the vested interests of politicians control the way resources are divided among constituents, and who the main recipients are of government handouts and funding.

But there is always the possibility of a negative outcome even to the most well-laid-out community project. For residents of Naledi, such drawbacks have only inspired them to continue searching for programmes that will further expand their village. The renovation of the local school as a result of a partnership between the village and EarthRise is one way in which Naledi has invested in the future of its children.

One of the first initiatives in Naledi was the construction of an eco-friendly multi-purpose centre that could serve as a crèche and a location for literacy and village meetings, a computer laboratory, a library, and a cultural centre for film study and drama. The centre functions as a facility in which young women and men from Naledi can increase their knowledge and learn new skills.

EarthRise also started a funding programme with donations from the lodge and international charities to enable the construction of a new school for village children. The previous school, built by the community some years before, was in bad shape and literally falling to pieces. Justine Rapulome, who has worked at the school for twenty years, holds the posts of principal, teacher, social worker, psychologist and general administrator, and teaches six grades in two classrooms. Her annual budget for the school is the equivalent of what a professional plumber in the city earns for two or three hours' work. Despite these constraints, this remarkable woman finds the strength and courage to go to work every day to educate the children of her village, knowing that this is the ultimate good she can do for them. 'This is the only way our children can succeed,' Rapulome emphasises. The inclusion of a crèche in Naledi's community centre has lifted a great weight off her shoulders, as she would usually have had to teach her future students the basics once they started school in addition to the rest of her syllabus. 'Most of the children arrive here for Grade One, not even knowing how to use a pencil,' she explains.

Naledi's new school was built by combining traditional construction methods of the Basotho with simple insulation technology that provides heat through environmentally friendly local materials, such as sawdust and wood shavings. It ensures that children are warm during the bitter mountain winters and cool in the summer, and all at a fraction of the usual cost of insulation. This was one of the community's approaches to eco-construction that would help take it into the twenty-first century.

Another innovation is the use of solar lamps by children when they study at home, which saves their families money usually spent on candles and kerosene. The use of solar power has reduced the threat of household fires in the village as well as the health consequences associated with regular inhalation of smoke and fumes. It has sparked a discussion among residents about creating a solar-driven village using more lamps, which Naledi has received through donations. Our shared vision is that Naledi will run on renewable energy for all its needs.

The elderly members of the community, a source of ancient wisdom and knowledge, are regularly consulted for their opinions on decisions and projects the village plans on undertaking. There is a lot of optimism in Naledi now, despite the many challenges they still face. Most of their hope stems from the clear plan they now have for their village's future success – which now seems achievable – and the direction they intend on taking to get there.

This is an important lesson for activists. *The poor are not victims.* They possess the resilience to feed their families every day on less money than the price of a bottle of water. In our dealings with them, we must show humility and patience. Building trust can take a long time, and this is integral if real change is to occur in a community. Decisions cannot be taken without their input, so we always avoid complexity in developing strategies for bolstering our movement. A series of small steps leads to small victories, and this is what ultimately inspires the confidence of the people. *Pole, pole.* Step by step.

When South Africa was reborn as a democracy in 1994, Anton Chaka, chair of the Naledi Village Committee, felt so hopeful that he did something everyone else in his village thought foolhardy: he built himself a house. While he knew there was a real possibility of it being bulldozed by a farmer, leaving him with only the windows and zinc roof, he would at least have the knowledge that he had once had a home of his own. He did not want to spend the rest of his life in a shack.

Now, over twenty years later, the village owns the land on which Chaka built his house. 'It ended up being a good bet,' he told me.

Real estate is always a bet, but before Naledi obtained the land on which Chaka's house was located, he might as well have built it on a rain cloud. There has always been fertile ground in this country for hope, but twenty-six years after Nelson Mandela walked free, South Africa is confronting a new era, one in which there are no 'big men' to save us. In this new world, we are forced to navigate uncertainties and difficulties by ourselves through innovation and protest. This is the only way we can secure a worthwhile life. Free but not free.

Many of the issues that even small villages like Naledi face are on a much broader, global level than what confronted anti-apartheid activists. Climate change is a phenomenon that is impacting negatively on communities even in remote, rural areas. Chaka has seen the effects of global warming in his village, and he is slowly learning to make sense of it.

'I have never understood the scientists talking about climate change,' he says. 'We have not had the benefit of proper education so we get lost when people talk about carbon emissions and all of the things we don't know. But we have seen this past year that rain has not fallen, the river is dry, the weather is very strange with heat waves and dust storms like we have never seen before in our lives. Now we can see the connection to climate change. And we know that although we have no electricity in the village, that somewhere people are doing bad things to Mother Earth that is affecting our lives here.'

Issues such as global warming have a bearing on how poor communities create their livelihoods, and only exacerbate the enormous struggles they experience every day. And while some residents have found the resources and designed the initiatives to forge a sustainable existence for themselves, the vast majority of South Africans have experienced little change in the material circumstances of their lives. Just obtaining the means to survive daily is regarded as a colossal feat by such people. They live from hand to mouth, dependent on handouts from government or piece jobs from the wealthy. Employment is sporadic or only a fantasy, and the resultant anger is legitimate and all-consuming.

The South African constitution and democracy has at its heart laws that demand social justice and human dignity for all: the right to nutritious food, clean water and quality education and health. We as citizens are justified in our attempts to demand freedom from poverty, violence and disease; it is our duty and privilege to hold to account the representatives of every level of political power. And our state institutions and national budget of a trillion rand – much more than we as apartheid activists had at our disposal – should be able to drive a strategy to transform lives and deliver the better life that was promised in 1994.

Communities such as Naledi in South Africa, Araku in India, Korail in Bangladesh and Kibera in Kenya have established their own cooperatives, savings groups, burial societies, sports clubs, cultural groups, housing projects, village committees and resident organisations. They have a vision of the future that has placed them and their children on a forward trajectory. Our role as activists is to walk with them and behind them, to share and co-create their plans for that future. However, true success, as Julius Nyerere emphasises, will only come when the people can say, 'We have done it for ourselves.'

In this realisation, Naledi can be said to be fully awake. 'You could say [we] got lucky,' Chaka says, 'but I don't think it's only that. We've worked hard down here. Slowly, slowly, everyone is changing, and with it our lives are changing for the better.'

With forty-two hectares of land that they can call their own, life for the Naledi residents is indeed changing. Now villagers can walk freely on the land, bury their loved ones in it, and do not need permission from a farmer to leave it if they want to.

Most importantly, they have secured a sustainable livelihood that has shown them what it truly means to live independently. Growing their own healthy food allows Naledi residents to feed themselves and their families, to assist the impoverished, and even to obtain profits through sales to other villages and the local market.

Some might say that such achievements are trivial; that struggling to reach the most basic level of existence is not an indication of future promise, but only of more anger and pain.

But Naledi's slow and steady transformation is just a small part of a larger theory of change. And the basis of this theory is, essentially, hard work and struggle. No community can win its power, and no government can learn to earn its power, unless a group of people can come together and fight for what matters to them. This kind of unity through action is what brings communities prosperity and the means of challenging abuses of power within their society. The prize is independence and authority in both the public and private spheres, and a refusal to be victimised by those with power and wealth. In such a context, communities have created their own wealth anyway – through activism, joint initiatives and solidarity. They are building their community assets one step at a time, and have stopped waiting for someone to help them. The villagers are no longer bystanders in determining their future.

The collaboration between EarthRise Trust and the village is one manifestation of the way activism and resourcefulness lead to transformative development. I know that there are thousands, if not millions, of people testing out such ideas too, looking for scalable and successful models of organisation that can be applied to their own causes or societal issues.

Perhaps the work EarthRise has done in Naledi will inspire something much bigger – a forest out of many disparate trees, a grand theory of transformation that can alter the world. Unfortunately, I have no such vision yet, although I do feel myself heading towards it, one village at a time.

We should keep in mind the Native American teaching that says, 'We have not inherited our planet from our ancestors. We have borrowed it from our children.'

It is the job of current activists to make the world a safer place for future generations, to ensure that they have dreams and ideals, not just anxiety and fear.

Activism is about positive disruption rather than working within a system. Every -ism works along a historical chain of events, and its adherents insist that it is the result of a logical and necessary progression. When the Soviet Union fell, capitalism presented itself as the inevitable destination of a long journey from socialism and isolationism. It proclaimed itself the End of History.

But what if we ended the End of History?

When I sat down with my comrades from EarthRise and our partners in the Naledi community, we tried to conceive of how this could be done. We had to analyse and reconsider the pattern that defined South African history and its many conflicts, and the two elements that we always came back to – which formed the central components of South Africa's colonial past and its record of exploitation – were people and the land.

We needed to find a way to disrupt this pattern, even if in a small but emphatic way. After three and a half centuries of colonial land grabs, racial segregation, capitalism and pollution, we realised something had to be done to reconcile the people with the resource most likely to restore some measure of power to them.

So to stop history from repeating itself in Naledi, we did the exact opposite of what colonial and apartheid oppressors have done in the past. We used the land for sustainable purposes, by preserving the environment, not destroying it. We had to uplift the people who had always been excluded from making full use of the land, reconnecting them with the soil and rock that contains their livelihood. Above all, we needed to make them feel proud, not ashamed, of who they were and where they came from. If EarthRise's work in Naledi has fulfilled any of these goals, then know we have succeeded.

This is my advice to those who want to inspire the same kind of hope in needy or impoverished communities. Change, while inevitable, can only occur when certain models or types are challenged and disrupted. But the overriding aim of this subversion should always be for the benefit of the community.

17

Ancient Wisdom
for Modern Times

I HAVE SPENT MOST of my life working with people who function on the fringes of society: hostel dwellers who formed the
backbone of the union movement; activists in informal settlements
hoping to inspire their neighbours into protest and action; and
members of poor rural villages trying to obtain even the smallest
shreds of dignity for their communities. Most of my cherished life
lessons have come from people like this, even though they generally lack any formal education. Many of them define who they are
by their place in a group; by the way their individual acts can be
inspired by and impact an entire culture or belief system.

The older I get, the more it resonates with me that much can
be learnt by looking at the world this way – from a shared moral
and cultural code. I strongly believe that teachings from indigenous
systems of thought have as much relevance for people trying to
adapt to modern ideas and events as they did thousands of years
ago. In fact, I would say that our salvation as a species relies on
tapping into and absorbing wisdom from ancient cultures, many of
which place what is natural or essential to life far above complex

reasoning and the models of accumulation and production that are prevalent today.

I am, of course, not referring to harmful cultural practices that are patriarchal, sexist, tribalist, racist or xenophobic.

To me, the indigenous cultures that possess the deepest, most profound ideas on finding your rightful place on the earth are those that revere it, and which display a deep gratitude to the planet for what it has given us and for everything we continue to take from it.

The Khoisan, the oldest human occupants of southern Africa and the world, have always expressed a deep love for the earth. The oldest gene pattern in modern humans exists in the San, and goes back 80 000 years. Their historical connection with the earth and its people is a long and rich one.

In 2015 I journeyed to Namibia with my son Kami, who was twenty-two at the time, and Pops Mohamed, the legendary musician who has spent much of his career studying the music and culture of the San. In Corridor 13, a dust bowl in the Kalahari Desert in the east of Namibia, I met !Gubi, a San shaman and one of the few remaining San knowledge holders of their ancient culture and practices. A wizened man of eighty-seven, !Gubi was born in Botswana and spent much of his life roaming the desert between his birthplace and Namibia, long before he needed to have a passport to make the journey. !Gubi's ancestors had done the same, some during a period when there were no other African tribes in the region. The arrival of white people with their guns and bibles in the seventeenth century marked the beginning of the extermination of the San. Today, after centuries of conflict both with white settlers and African tribes, the San and many of the traditions upholding their hunter-gatherer lifestyle have virtually been wiped out from modern southern African history.

!Gubi regards the modern emphasis on competition and conquest as the reason for the isolation that exists between different societies. Instead of focusing on what we can give and share with the world, we choose instead to prioritise what we can get out of it. 'Humanity is losing its way,' he observes. 'We do not hold each other together and share our humanity. We live in disharmony. God is sad that we do not respect Mother Nature. We do not respect the forests, our land, water, the wild animals and our plants in which God lives.'

Humans have indeed become divorced from the earth, indifferent to how much care it needs for us to continue living on it. Industrialisation induces us to live on top of one another, but the design of our societies – identical boxy houses and apartment blocks, high thick walls separating the wealthy from the impoverished – prevents us from appreciating valuable human connections, or the beauty and splendour contained in the natural world. Roads crammed with cars spewing poisonous gas, filthy overpopulated cities, oceans and sea animals covered in spilled oil, and an ever-increasing list of endangered animals – these are the remnants of the modern-day human connection with the earth. And we feel disconnected from one another too, even with technology that makes us the most connected generation in the history of humanity. The momentary happiness we obtain with the attainment of material goods trumps our love for the planet that has given us the ultimate gift: life.

If we are to figure out how to restore the earth's lost beauty and health, we need to consider how humans lived here before we invented tools that could destroy it. Indigenous peoples like the San hold the answers to this question, I believe. Thousands of years of knowledge about surviving nature's challenges belong now to just a small group of individuals in a few remote societies scattered around the world.

These are the people more desperate to save our planet than anyone else. They regard the whole universe, including nature and all the living beings in our world, as manifestations of the divine. The San do not kill for pleasure but for survival, believing that God is contained in all living things. Nature is the divine force that has nourished and maintained them for thousands of years, and to lose a connection to the land is, essentially, to lose who they are.

I sensed the pain of this growing separation of the San from the earth every time !Gubi spoke to me about his history. In his long life !Gubi has suffered through numerous political, social and legal changes that have weakened the San's relationship with the land and their ability to move over it freely as their ancestors did. Borders, fences, passports, citizenship and private property have no place in the nomadic San culture, but are integral for peaceful relations between countries and communities in modern times. By imposing these laws and customs on the San, southern African governments have essentially taken away their freedom. The governments are no different from the colonists who infringed on the San's liberties in an attempt to 'civilise' them.

We should do everything we can to assimilate the San's reverence for nature and their knowledge of its secrets before both are lost. Teaching our children to live off the land will show them how much it has given us and reinforce the notion that all living things, including people, are deserving of respect. It is painful to witness the anger, frustration and discontent that exists among our youth as they protest their growing marginalisation from society. But helping to adjust their perspectives of what constitutes happiness with the beliefs of the San might alleviate some of the despair they are experiencing. Living simply and showing empathy for others will weaken our regard for money and worthless objects, increasing instead our respect for the things that make *people* valuable: their diversity and cultures, their language and experience. Governments need to start acknowledging the worth of ancient cultures if they hope to foster unity among the multitude of other cultures, ethnicities and religions that make up most modern societies today. North America's fraught relationship with its aboriginal populations provides a powerful example of the way modern industrial ideology infringes on the customs and beliefs of indigenous peoples, even in supposedly democratic settings. In July 2013 I visited Grand Rapids, Manitoba, and discussed the destructive effects that industrialisation was having on Canada's First Nations communities with Ovide Mercredi, their former national chief.

Mercredi's community is struggling to deal with the ecological and cultural impact of a Manitoba Hydro dam that was constructed on their sacred burial grounds in 1968. Not only is the community still dealing with limited access to electricity fifty years after the hydroelectric dam was built, but the dam, trespassing on a space that is revered by the First Nations community, is also a symbol of the degradation and ruin that Western societies have inflicted on Native American culture through the centuries. Having been dispossessed of their tribal lands, the First Nations are now struggling to hold on to their beliefs as well.

Like !Gubi does for the San, Mercredi yearns for a time when the First Nations people could practise their traditions and experience the wonder of nature without the constraints of industrialisation and Western laws.

Now his people are subject to the many vices and socio-economic problems with which modern American people have to grapple. 'We struggle against poverty,' Mercredi laments, 'the social disintegration that destroys our communities as drugs, alcohol and junk food hold our youth in a deadly embrace.'

There is little in indigenous American culture that would allow for such behaviour from youth, mostly because the elements that encourage it – recreational drug-taking or overconsumption of junk food – were uncommon in ancient societal practices. It is therefore difficult for community leaders like Mercredi to find recourse in their culture for reforming First Nations youths, many of whom have adopted the ideas and values of modern American culture. 'What choice do we have?' Mercredi asks. 'The dominant model of dealing with poverty is capitalistic – gas stations, casinos, mining and oil exploration. But these are in contradiction to our way of life [which is] living in harmony with Mother Earth.'

Mercredi still values the philosophy espoused by the iconic Suquamish and Duwamish leader Chief Seattle:

> How can you buy or sell the sky, the warmth of the land? The idea is strange to us.... We can only protect the land, not own it. Earth does not belong to us; we belong to Mother Earth. There is no quiet place in the white man's cities, no place to hear the leaves of spring or the rustle of insects' wings. Perhaps it is because I am a savage and do not understand, but the clatter only seems to insult my ears.

In the belief system of the First Nations, the Great Spirit, or Kitche Manitou, 'inhabits all things – mountains, trees, water, air, animals, plants and humans. It is a sacred bond based on the foundations of sharing and caring; honesty and truth; kindness and love; and strength and courage.' While Mercredi emphasises that the gods of the First Nations are not vengeful or frightening, the prominent role that they play in nature makes disrespecting it a sacrilegious offence.

There is a clear link between forgetting or disregarding the wisdom of ancient cultures and the contamination and disrespect of our natural environment. Thousands of years ago indigenous peoples, the first humans to walk in nature, saw the earth as a manifestation of the divine. But with Western encroachment and even takeover of certain values, many cultures have placed these broad and all-encompassing beliefs into one narrow view of development – one that privileges a love of stuff before the loyalty we owe the earth and other life. Nature and its gifts are seen as mere conduits for making fleeting or destructive material goods. And as more people are born and human demand for resources exceeds our planetary limits, it has become imperative for us to return to social frameworks that advance our knowledge of the earth's significance and value.

We should not be prisoners of our past, but we can learn from the good in order to be liberators of our future. Africa is not only the storehouse of humanity, but a continent rich in gifts from the earth. Everything that makes us human, from walking upright, cognitive thinking, language and art to the earliest tools and even agriculture, comes from our continent. We could choose to use the many resources at our disposal for something worthwhile and good rather than to uphold an insidious, outdated system of wealth creation that has made us greedier, less healthy and poorer. Africa has been and still is a link to civilisation and to evolving to a higher purpose. And this purpose has always been our people, whether to free them from the shackles of hate and anger, or to unite them in a struggle against a common enemy. The African principle of *ubuntu* – 'I am, because we are' – has more relevance than ever before. It is not based on modern philanthropic notions of giving, but on sharing, caring and solidarity.

For too long indigenous knowledge systems have been crushed under the waves of slavery, colonisation and neoliberalism. We need to reclaim the centrality of all types of knowledge today to chart a new way forward for the way we think. It is time to go back to the point when solidarity and compassion, and not a love of money or things, drove our actions and the regard we showed for all our people.

18

Where to from Here?

A S I STOOD on the peak of Kilimanjaro, the highest point in Africa, I imagined the continent as a bright star in a constellation of global chaos.

Africa should be a global superpower, so why isn't it?

By 2050 there will be nearly two and half billion people on the continent. More than half will be under twenty-five, the majority of the world's population of youth.[1] When many developed countries' populations are ageing, most people in African countries will be in their peak, ready – if we prepare them – to take on challenges that activists in our generation failed to overcome.

The vast quantity of natural resources at our disposal provides another means for Africa to play a central role in shaping a new global economy, but this time through a paradigm that places human value before material value. To do this we must start prioritising the needs of our own people and respecting our environmental and planetary boundaries – something that should not be too hard to achieve. Africa possesses close to 60 per cent of the world's remaining uncultivated land, which covers a fifth of the land surface, and our forests, rivers and oceans are rich sources of food and life. It is inconceivable that nearly a third of the world's hungry people live in Africa and that half of all childhood deaths occur on the continent (a number expected to rise to 70 per cent by the middle of the century). With so much natural wealth right under our feet, it is difficult to come to terms with the fact that half of the people in sub-Saharan Africa live on less than $1.90 per day.[2]

The factor holding us back the most is the inability of African governments and leaders to promote unity and empathy among their people.

I have been a social activist for over four decades. In this time I have learnt that fighting for social justice and even changing the system is not enough to build a worthwhile world for our children to live in. The people who will lead them and guide them to their futures need to change too. And all too often even the most outstanding leaders can be co-opted and corrupted once they gain access to wealth and power.

To shift the consciousness of communities, populations and the entire human species, we have to do the same for those who have the most influence over them.

Most of our leaders are so desperate to cling to power that they are completely out of touch with their people. They govern their countries like medieval rulers, as individual fiefdoms on a mass of land with fifty-three other fiefdoms. Nations in the rest of the world take full advantage of their alliances and relationships with their neighbours, strengthening their trade dealings and allowing for easier transfer of knowledge, goods, services and people. Africa in the meanwhile, with its vast store of ancient knowledge systems, has discarded these tools for promoting unity for more divergent schools of thought.

Africa's growth should not just be dependent on global commodity and crude-oil price rises and slumps. If African countries combined their strength and wealth, we would have the bargaining power to negotiate trade agreements based on what our people need and want, and not be subject to the laws of trading blocs in the European Union, United States, China, India, Russia and Brazil.

Mo Ibrahim, a mobile-technology entrepreneur and one of Africa's wealthiest people, is an old friend of mine who has a long history of showing faith in the continent and investing in its enterprises. In the mid-nineties, when Mo discovered that overseas investors were too afraid to invest in countries outside of South Africa, Tunisia and Egypt, he sold his mobile-technology business in Europe and established the pan-African operator Celtel. He refused to pay a single bribe to grow his company, and continues to speak out against international businesses receiving incentives from African governments to invest in their countries: 'Businesspeople must take the risk,' he avers. 'Why does a business need government to subsidise their risk in Africa? Do they ask for such in Europe or the United States?'

In 2006 Mo set up the Mo Ibrahim Foundation, of which I am a board member. The foundation aims to advance development in Africa by promoting good governance and excellent leadership. It has helped intensify Mo's rally cry for African nations to create decent jobs and improve their economies by utilising the vast store of resources available to them. 'We do not understand our strength as the fastest-growing telecommunications market in the world,' he says. 'We have 750 million users today. Do we have a single telecommunications equipment supplier on the continent?'

Mo points out that such a phenomenon would be unheard of in China, where the government forces companies to create manufacturing plants that hire Chinese people and train them with appropriate skills. Africa, in contrast, is 'only a supplier of raw materials. Our African intellectual resources end up in the developed world, strengthening the stranglehold global companies have [on] us. Our countries become markets for manufactured goods and services from developed economies.'

Little is being done on the continent to bring this exploitation of our resources by foreign economies to an end. The African Union frequently espouses its bold vision of Agenda 2063, which aims to increase the continent's self-reliance by mobilising its citizens, taking full advantage of our resources and promoting unity among all fifty-four nations. But so far this initiative has only been laid out on paper, with very few countries showing the drive or capability to implement this strategy in reality.

A new African narrative requires a transformation in the matrix of our development. Africans have been sold a myth. The neoliberal dogma that controls the current world economic system is unsustainable, deepening the inequality swelling the ranks of the global underclass. Today that class is revolting against the establishment, expressing its rage at governments that have forfeited sovereignty to corporate power and allowed transnationals to destroy their natural environment for the material wants of overseas consumers.

In the rest of the world, the effects of globalisation and growing unemployment are causing discord even in developed economies. The West is seeing a rise in extreme right-wing politics, as manifested in the election of Donald Trump as US president and the upsurge of rightist populism in Europe. On the other side of the world, the growing popularity of extremist movements in Africa and the Middle East offers an equally disturbing counterfoil to the current state of world politics. The efforts of citizens in these regions to resist such currents are suppressed by powerful surveillance states intent on closing off the civic and political space.

But activists should not give up in the face of this tyranny. The coming together of masses of people to protest a shared injustice is what has won so many countries their freedom. It continues to be the most powerful weapon people can employ to keep fighting inequality and exploitation.

Our new mass struggle should be about holding our governments to account and ensuring that their rule makes a positive difference for all citizens. In Africa, solving our development problems is the key to solving them everywhere else. And we do this by recognising the advantages of operating from a lower base in world economic and political development. Instead of repeating mistakes that have been made elsewhere, we can learn from them. We can leapfrog into a development paradigm that is economically and socially inclusive, and which obtains its power from ancient knowledge, wisdom and culture.

We could kick-start a new way of creating harmony between ourselves, other species and the planet, fixing our energy crisis while fighting global warming through the use of renewable energy for a just energy future. We can begin working within our planetary boundaries by taking enough to care for our species and preserving the rest for future generations. A joint campaign against hunger and aimed at creating sustainable livelihoods could help us end malnutrition and promote healthy diets in Africa, while feeding the rest of the world as well.

Villages like Naledi are our models for creating more self-sustaining communities that grow their own food, raise their incomes and keep them circulating in the local economy. In the whole of Africa 70 per cent of food is produced by women subsistence farmers, while agriculture generates 57 per cent of the continent's jobs, making it the main source of income for 90 per cent of the rural population.[3] If we can supply women farmers with the tools that they need to expand their businesses – legal titles to land, financial support for building seed banks, irrigation and access to power – entire villages and cities could become food secure.

African countries need to formulate entrepreneurial models that will assist villages and communities in finding their own means of generating socially useful goods and services. From the village to the peri-urban and the urban, organisations and activists have to start steering innovation towards the pivotal idea of livelihoods. The role of government is to provide land and resources and to open the market to communities' surplus crops so that they can assure their own futures.

Our youth population is a powerful force for speeding up and demanding change. They are the spark that will fire up the real 'All Africans Rising' narrative instead of a small elite at the top. Around the world, many social and political movements are driven by young people who obtain their power from social media and by being the most connected generation in the history of humanity.

The digital revolution is inspiring a move away from manual labour towards robotics, 3D printing and nanotechnology. It is redefining economic growth, work and business models in every sector. We have seen huge growth in the arts and creative sectors involving music and culture because of the rise in internet usage. Individuals and smaller groups now have access to channels that can help them appeal to wide markets all across the planet without the barriers of scope and scale that the pre-digital period would have imposed on them. In Africa, we need to find ways to start using this technology to redesign our education and health systems, which are in desperate need of improvement.

This is where people like Sam Pitroda come in. Entrepreneur, inventor and engineer, Sam is a close family friend who has taught me just how much potential there is for generating widespread transformation through the use of technology. Sam has over a hundred patents to his name, and his commitment to closing the digital divide is unparalleled with anything else I have ever seen. Much of India's information technology revolution was inspired by him following his work in the eighties, when he launched the Centre for Development of Telematics (C-DOT) to escalate the growth of digital communications in India, even in remote villages like the one in which he was born. Similar to other developmental organisations I have discussed in this book, Sam is harnessing cutting-edge technology to drive progress on a range of other issues relating to water, literacy, immunisation, oil, seeds and dairy.

Sam's argument is that developing countries need to 'redesign the world' by creating economies that are inclusive and circular. 'We have to dream big, beyond the limitation of our current ideologies and mindsets,' Sam stresses. 'But we are led by leaders without imagination and tied by the umbilical cord to vested interests that make super profits from the status quo.'

Some of these 'big dreams' can include harnessing green energy through solar, wind and geothermal sources to rapidly replace old poisonous technology that makes use of fossil fuels, nuclear power and fracking.

The question is where to begin organising such an outcome. Given the state of our environment and the economies of many developed nations, it is clear that we cannot continue ignoring such questions any longer. We need a meaningful commitment to a set of global organising principles and a model for the world we want. And it should be obvious by now that the change will not come from our leaders, who seem to feel no urgency to act on the promises they made during election season.

Instead they attend global summits where very few real decisions are taken. Or they hire international development organisations that have become risk averse and build endless checks and balances to avoid failing in their attempts to solve social and economic issues.

It is up to social movements to demand, shape and expand a paradigm of sustainable growth and a just means of transitioning into it.

We have to build a new world, one constituency at a time. Whether it be your village, university, workplace, home or place of faith, change begins in the community, through people coming together to switch direction and create alternative methods of functioning in the world.

If we had to write a list of the vital needs and rights of every person on the planet, especially young children, the task should not be too difficult or complex to complete. Every person should be able to love and be loved; to live in safety and shelter; and to have food, health and education in order to realise their full potential. We should not be measuring our progress by GDP growth, but rather learn to draw on the extraordinary richness of our culture and the *ubuntu* way of life. We must embrace our shared humanity, begin living in harmony with nature and appreciate the lessons taught to us by the 'Great Spirit' that lives in everything that surrounds us. In other words, we have to spiritualise our individual lives to consider a different way of living – one that treasures harmony and promotes tolerance of the world's magnificent diversity.

I am exhausted by the shallowness, by the selfish and egotistical values handed down by Western civilisation as the keys to fulfilment and obtaining popularity. Instead of seeing money and material goods as the ultimate source of wealth, perhaps we should begin looking at it differently, the way Bhutan does. This beautiful country in the Himalayas measures happiness not by GDP wealth but by GNH – 'gross national happiness'.

To bring contentment and nourishment to all members of our society, we should consider creating powerful coalitions at both local and global levels. We must begin holding so-called world and business leaders to account for their crimes against humanity and the planet. We can achieve this by organising around our rights to freedom of speech and assembly in order to protest against abuses of power. We have to start defending the civic space.

The failure of political will at the top is the result of our failure to organise at the bottom. Politicians respond to power, and right now the only power they bow to is that of corporations and the wealthy. Their masters make up the class of elites that is bereft of values and indifferent to the suffering they have inflicted on millions of others.

As activists and responsible citizens we must know not just what we are against, but what we are for. True wisdom, it is said, resides in the collective rather than the individual. Leaders can be found in our communities, in the places that many have not even thought to look. We cannot be saved by individuals or messiahs, but by the just actions of all, whether or not you are poor, uneducated or without a job.

Poverty, inequality and the large-scale spread of disease are overwhelmingly political constructs. To fight bad politics, activists and movements need to embrace ethics and begin taking informed but calculated political risks to navigate areas of difficulty that our governments choose to overlook or ignore. We have to turn the sword on its former wielder. Fundamental development in society cannot be achieved by a technical and apolitical strategy.

I learnt this when I started working in the harsh world of politics. But my most valuable lessons have come from ordinary people and organisations that have spent their lives, like I have, fighting against the status quo.

Now humanity is standing at yet another crossroads. To figure out which road to take, we have to realise that it is not one that can be walked only by individuals or select groups or societies. We have to learn what it means to share a world with other people, to manage conflict and create bonds of friendship that will enlarge our capacity for tolerance of social and biological diversity.

Just because you can say you are free at last, does not mean that your freedom will last. Freedom can be as fleeting as the wind. It needs to be rekindled, rededicated, reinvigorated and defended daily from power-drunk leaders and greedy corporations.

Change revolves around a lynchpin – a simple idea, a signature image, a conclusive act. That lynchpin idea is the spark, and the spark just needs a tinder of dissent in order to catch light. You, the next generation, have to find the spark for this new world.

As I enter the last part of my life, I can see how much my past has prepared me for the new challenges in my future. I feel ready because I know that the toughest journey is the one every person takes on the road to discovering their real worth and power.

All of this power, as a collective force, is needed to bring about a different beginning now that the old way of living and thinking is dying. It is power that has to be exerted with courage and urgency if we hope to build the new outside the old system.

I once experienced the joy and optimism of living in a new world, of winning freedom. But now pessimism and a lack of imagination are steadily replacing the hope that liberty once bestowed on us.

We have to start dreaming again of a new start. We need to abolish the bitterness in our hearts and turn our anger into a tool that will forge peace, compassion, reconciliation and justice. If we want to practise our right to walk on this earth, we have to acknowledge that it is the earth that has given us this right in the first place.

There are clearly many more Kilimanjaros to climb before real freedom can be achieved. But one thing remains the prerogative, and that is to never give up the struggle for human dignity. Nelson Mandela, the founding father of our democracy, recognised this double-edged quality of freedom. He knew that unless freedom was constantly fought for, its worth eternally valued, it could quickly be lost:

> I have walked that long road to freedom. I have tried not to falter; I have made missteps along the way. But I have discovered the secret that after climbing a great hill, one only finds that there are many more hills to climb. I have taken a moment here to rest, to steal a view of the glorious vista that surrounds me, to look back on the distance I have come. But I can only rest for a moment, for with freedom come responsibilities, and I dare not linger, for my long walk is not ended.

One step at a time. *Pole, pole.* Old battles renewed. New battles to be fought.

We all want to live in peace, harmony and love where the rights of all human beings and Mother Earth are respected as part of our daily reality. There is only one way to achieve that goal: CHANGE!

Acknowledgements

I AM ETERNALLY GRATEFUL to all my teachers, many of them extraordinary trade union, community, political and spiritual leaders, who have instilled in me the human values that guide me today.

I thank my ancestors, especially my mother, for sharing their wisdom with me and even today guiding my thoughts and actions.

I am indebted to all – too many to list here – who have selflessly shepherded me throughout my life in my pursuit of truth and given me meaning.

I am emboldened daily by the love and compassion of the mother of my children, my wife and soulmate Lucie Pagé, who has always stood beside me with words of encouragement that cast a light on my journey of life.

Finally, I want to acknowledge Gaia, Mother Earth, the source of all life in our world, and thank the Divine who guides us in the Universe.

JAY NAIDOO
JANUARY 2017

Abbreviations

ANC: African National Congress
BCM: Black Consciousness Movement
BPC: Black People's Convention
BRAC: Bangladesh Rural Advancement Committee
BRICS: Brazil, Russia, India, China and South Africa
CODESA: Convention for a Democratic South Africa
COSATU: Congress of South African Trade Unions
CUT: Central Única dos Trabalhadores
FOSATU: Federation of South African Trade Unions
GDP: gross domestic product
GNU: Government of National Unity
IFP: Inkatha Freedom Party
IMF: International Monetary Fund
MDM: Mass Democratic Movement
MK: Umkhonto we Sizwe
MP: member of parliament
NGO: non-governmental organisation
NPA: National Peace Accord
NUM: National Union of Mineworkers
PAC: Pan Africanist Congress
PT: Partido dos Trabalhadores (Brazil's Workers' Party)

RDP: Reconstruction and Development Programme
SACP: South African Communist Party
SASO: South African Students' Organisation
SHOFCO: Shining Hope for Communities
UCT: University of Cape Town
UDF: United Democratic Front
UNEP: United Nations Environment Programme
UWUSA: United Workers' Union of South Africa

Notes

The Summit
1. *Uhuru* is the Kiswahili word for 'freedom'.
2. '62 people own the same as half the world, reveals Oxfam Davos report' (Oxfam, January 2017), https://www.oxfam.org/en/pressroom/pressreleases/2016-01-18/62-people-own-same-half-world-reveals-oxfam-davos-report, last accessed 27 January 2017.
3. United Nations, 'The Millennium Development Goals Report' (New York: 2015), http://www.un.org/millenniumgoals/2015_MDG_Report/pdf/MDG=%202015%20rev%20(July%201).pdf, p. 6, last accessed 25 November 2016.

Race to the Bottom
1. 'Forced Removals', *Overcoming Apartheid*, http://overcomingapartheid.msu.edu/multimedia.php?id=65-259-6, last accessed 25 November 2016.

The Spark
1. TheDayDawnedRed, 'Steve Biko – rare TV interview', 30 October 2010, *YouTube*, https://www.youtube.com/watch?v=JNmAcgdO2Ck, last accessed 25 November 2016.

Organise or Starve
1. The history of the black union movement in South Africa goes back to 1919, when the Industrial and Commercial Union was formed by Clements Kadalie.

The Objective Objective
1. 'Leon Trotsky', *Wikiquotes*, https://en.wikiquote.org/wiki/Leon_Trotsky, last accessed 12 December 2016.

2. Jerelyn Eddings, 'ANC admits committing brutality Mandela calls acts "inexcusable"', *The Baltimore Sun*, 20 October 1992, http://articles.baltimoresun .com/1992-10-20/news/1992294166_1_anc-military-south-africa-abuses, last accessed 25 November 2016.

Building Solidarity

1. Bretton Woods is a city in New Hampshire, United States, where the Bretton Woods Agreements, which launched an international monetary system and led to the creation of the IMF, were concluded in 1944.
2. Adeyemi Adepetun, 'Africa's mobile phone penetration now 67%', *The Guardian* (Nigeria), 17 June 2015, http://guardian.ng/technology/africas-mobile-phone -penetration-now-67/, last accessed 25 November 2016.
3. Richard Dobbs et al., 'The world at work: Jobs, pay, and skills for 3.5 billion people', *Report: McKinsey Global Institute* (McKinsey&Company: June 2012), http://www.mckinsey.com/global-themes/employment-and-growth/the-world -at-work, last accessed 25 November 2016.
4. 'Workforce', *Wikipedia*, https://en.wikipedia.org/wiki/Workforce, last accessed 25 November 2016; Asia-Plus, '40 per cent of the global workforce reportedly works in the informal economy', 13 June 2014, http://news.tj/en/ news/40-cent-global-workforce-reportedly-works-informal-economy, last accessed 25 November 2016.

The Challenge of Democracy

1. 'The youth should draw inspiration from Chris Hani', *NUMSA News*, 5 July 2013, http://www.numsa.org.za/article/the-youth-should-draw-inspiration -from-chris-hani-2013-07-05/, last accessed 12 December 2016.
2. '3 richest South Africans have wealth equal to the poorest 28 million' – Oxfam (January 2017), http://www.702.co.za/articles/239288/3-richest-south- africans-have-wealth-equal-to-the-poorest-28-million-oxfam, last accessed 27 January 2017.

Lessons of the Lula Moment

1. Patrick Gillespie, 'Brazil crisis: Economy spirals deeper into recession', 1 June 2016, *CNN Money*, http://money.cnn.com/2016/06/01/news/economy/ brazil-recession-economy/, last accessed 25 November 2016.
2. 'BRICS', *Wikipedia*, https://en.wikipedia.org/wiki/BRICS, last accessed 25 November 2016.

Organising for a Planet

1. 'Niger Delta', *Wikipedia*, https://en.wikipedia.org/wiki/Niger_Delta#Nigerian _oil, last accessed 25 November 2016.
2. Ruth Krause, 'Oil spills keep devastating Niger Delta', *Deutsche Welle*, http://www.dw.com/en/oil-spills-keep-devastating-niger-delta/a-18327732, last accessed 25 November 2016.

3. 'Niger Delta', *Wikipedia.*
4. Godwin Uyi Ojo, 'Shell, Rumuekpe clan soaked in crude oil, Nigeria', *Environmental Justice Atlas,* https://ejatlas.org/conflict/shell-rumuekpe-clan-soaked-in-crude-oil-nigeria, last accessed 25 November 2016.
5. 'Factsheet: Shell's environmental devastation in Nigeria', *Center for Constitutional Rights,* 24 March 2009, https://ccrjustice.org/home/get-involved/tools-resources/fact-sheets-and-faqs/factsheet-shells-environmental-devastation, last accessed 25 November 2016.
6. John Vidal, 'Niger delta oil spill clean-up launched – but could take quarter of a century', *The Guardian,* 2 June 2016, https://www.theguardian.com/global-development/2016/jun/02/niger-delta-oil-spill-clean-up-launched-ogoniland-communities-1bn, last accessed 25 November 2016.
7. World Wide Fund for Nature, 'Living Planet Report 2016', http://wwf.panda.org/about_our_earth/all_publications/lpr_2016/, p. 18, last accessed 25 November 2016.
8. 'NASA, NOAA Data Show 2016 Warmest Year on Record Globally' (January 2017), https://www.nasa.gov/press-release/nasa-noaa-data-show-2016-warmest-year-on-record-globally, last accessed 27 January 2017.
9. 'IEA says INDCs will slow energy emissions growth dramatically', *UN Climate Change Newsroom,* http://newsroom.unfccc.int/unfccc-newsroom/iea-says-pledges-for-cop21-slow-energy-emissions-growth-dramatically/, last accessed 25 November 2016.
10. Damian Carrington, 'Leave fossil fuels buried to prevent climate change, study urges', *The Guardian,* 7 January 2015, https://www.theguardian.com/environment/2015/jan/07/much-worlds-fossil-fuel-reserve-must-stay-buried-prevent-climate-change-study-says, last accessed 25 November 2016.
11. Laura Merrill et al., 'Tackling fossil fuel subsidies and climate change: Levelling the energy playing field', http://norden.diva-portal.org/smash/get/diva2:860647/FULLTEXT02.pdf, p. 11, last accessed 25 November 2016.
12. 'Pricing Carbon', *The World Bank,* http://www.worldbank.org/en/programs/pricing-carbon, last accessed 25 November 2016.
13. Norimitsu Onishi, 'Windmills or reactor cores? Inside South Africa's energy clash', *New York Times,* 13 November 2016, http://www.nytimes.com/2016/11/14/world/africa/south-africa-energy-solar-wind-nuclear.html, last accessed 25 November 2016.
14. Trust Matsilele, 'Sub-Saharan Africa sees unrivalled growth in mobile banking', *CNBCAfrica,* 19 February 2016, http://www.cnbcafrica.com/news/special-report/2016/02/19/mobile-banking-mpesa-moodys/, last accessed 25 November 2016.
15. Samantha Spooner, '600,000 deaths caused in Africa by lack of electricity, but continent has huge untapped "green jobs" potential', *Mail & Guardian Africa,* 5 June 2015, http://mgafrica.com/article/2015-05-28-renewable-energy-employment-africa, last accessed 25 November 2016.

The Right to Feel Human

1. Lee Mwiti, 'These new facts about Africa's population will simply blow you away', *Mail & Guardian Africa*, 13 August 2014, http://mgafrica.com/article/2014-08-13-these-new-facts-about-africas-population-will-simply-blow-you-away, last accessed 25 November 2016.

The Naledi Star

1. '3 richest South Africans have wealth equal to the poorest 28 million' – Oxfam (January 2017), http://www.702.co.za/articles/239288/3-richest-south-africans-have-wealth-equal-to-the-poorest-28-million-oxfam, last accessed 27 January 2017.

Where to from Here?

1. 'Projections of population growth', *Wikipedia*, https://en.wikipedia.org/wiki/Projections_of_population_growth, last accessed 25 November 2016.
2. Maura K. Leary, 'Poverty Overview', *The World Bank*, http://www.worldbank.org/en/topic/poverty/overview, last accessed 25 November 2016.
3. 'Women and agriculture in sub-Saharan Africa', *Wikipedia*, https://en.wikipedia.org/wiki/Women_and_agriculture_in_Sub-Saharan_Africa, last accessed 25 November 2016.

Index

!Gubi 202–204

Abed, Sir Fazle Hasan 134, 138–139
acid rain 145, 147
activism 2–4, 24, 79–80, 86, 199, 212
Africa 9–11, 127, 207, 209–214
African National Congress *see* ANC
Africans Rising 171
African Union 211–212
Afrigrow 192
Afrikaans language 40, 41
Agenda 2063 211–212
agriculture *see* farming industry
Akhter, Nazma 141–142
Akiba Mashinani 160, 162–163
Akingol, Maria 145–146
alcohol abuse 130–131
America *see* United States of America
Anatomy of Revolution, The 48
ANC
    campaign of defiance 31
    banned 39
    MK 62–63, 71
    use of force 62–63
    union movement 50, 53
    COSATU and 85, 104–108, 110, 118
    unbanned 95–96
    elections 110
    GNU 104
    as ruling party 109, 117

anger 2, 32, 37, 41–42, 72, 74, 142, 218
Annan, Kofi 153–154
apartheid
    JN's experiences of 12, 19–24, 37–38,
        187–189
    resistance against 29–30, 62–63, 68,
        73–75, 83, 95, 188
Arab Spring uprisings 23–24, 43–44, 80
Araku, India 123–132, 197
arms industries 73
Art of War, The 48, 73
arts sector 214

Bangladesh 133–143, 197
Bangladesh Rural Advancement
    Committee *see* BRAC
banking system 78–81
Bantustans 21
Barayi, Elijah 87
Bassey, Nnimmo 147
BCM *see* Black Consciousness
    Movement
BEE *see* black economic empowerment
Berlin Wall, fall of 67, 101
Bhutan 216
Biko, Stephen Bantu (Steve) 26–30, 34, 37,
    42, 49, 74, 168
Black Consciousness Movement (BCM)
    25–30, 48, 49, 86
black economic empowerment 174

Black People's Convention *see* BPC
Boipatong massacre 98
Boko Haram 72
Bouazizi, Mohamed 23
BPC 49
BRAC 134–139
Brazil 25, 111–119
breastfeeding 136–137
Breivik, Anders Behring 72
Bretton Woods institutions *see* IMF;
    World Bank
Brexit 70
BRICS 114–115
Brinton, Crane 48
burning down of facilities 64–65, 90–91

Cairo, Egypt 42–44
Campaign of Defiance against Unjust
    Laws 95, 185
Canada's First Nations communities
    205–206
capitalism 20, 65–67, 77–79, 189–190, 199
carbon credits 128
carbon emissions *see* greenhouse gas
    emissions
carbon tax 155
C-DOT 214
cellphones *see* mobile technology
Celtel 211
Central Intelligence Agency 62
Central Única dos Trabalhadores
    see CUT
Centre for Development of Telematics
    see C-DOT
Chaka, Anton 195–197
Chebbi, Aya 23
children *see* youth
China 13–14, 77–78, 211
    see also BRICS
CIA 62
clean energy 154–155
climate change 34–35, 66, 145, 149–158, 196
    see also global warming
clinic for mothers, Kenya 167
clothing industry 139–143
coalition building 89–90

CODESA 100–101
coffee farming 126, 128–129
Cold War 62, 77
colonialism 20–22, 33–34
commodification 12, 22, 66, 128, 190
communism 49, 67–68, 77
competitiveness 66
Congress of South African Trade Unions
    see COSATU
connections with other people 10–11,
    203–204, 214, 217
constitution of South Africa 100–101
consumerism 65–67, 142–143
Convention for a Democratic South
    Africa *see* CODESA
corruption 52, 106, 112, 114, 180, 182
COSATU
    alliances 85–87, 89–90, 118
    ANC and 85, 104–108, 110, 118
    Defiance Campaign 185
    establishment of 83–84, 184
    GNU 104–108
    IFP and 90, 97
    Soviet Union visit 68
    strategies of 16, 31–32, 73, 75, 81–82,
        84–88, 91–93, 125, 128, 191–192
    use of force 62–63
    UWUSA and 87
creative sector 214
crony capitalism 15
cultural barriers 57–58, 92
CUT 118

decolonisation 33–34
Defiance Campaign *see* Campaign of
    Defiance against Unjust Laws
De Klerk, F.W. 91, 95
Delivery Centre 134–138
democracy 103–110
development sector 121–122, 182
Dhaka, Bangladesh *see* Korail,
    Bangladesh; Rana Plaza disaster
diseases 161, 216–217
donors 52, 64, 79, 121
Doo, Eric 148
Dutra, Olívio 116, 118

Earth Charter 152
EarthRise Mountain Lodge 181–182
EarthRise Trust 175–183, 186,
    190–200
Earth Summit of 1992 149, 152
economic growth 13–14
education *see* schools
Egypt 42–44
elections
    1994, first democratic 103
    2016, municipal 110
entrepreneurship 138, 166–167, 191–192,
    213
environment, importance of 14, 66,
    145–149, 203, 206–207, 213, 216
European Enlightenment 22
evictions 19–20, 182, 187
extinctions 150–151
extremist groups 73, 212
Eye of the Needle, The 49

factory labourers 50, 140–141
'Fallist' movement 33, 80
Fanon, Frantz 48
farming industry 114, 125–129, 173–174,
    191–192, 209, 213
Federation of South African Trade
    Unions *see* FOSATU
#FeesMustFall movement 33
FIFA World Cup 117
financial crisis of 2008 79–81
    see also recessions
First Nations 205–206
forced removals 19–20, 182, 187
FOSATU 51–56, 84
freedom 6–8, 17, 172, 217–218
Freedom Charter 63, 106, 174
Freire, Paulo 48
Friedman, Milton 66–67

Gandhi, Mahatma 31, 130, 151
garment industry 139–143
gas extraction 147
GEAR (Growth, Employment and
    Redistribution) 107
genetically modified crops 127

global warming 14, 35, 145–146, 150–158,
    196, 213
    see also climate change
GNU 103–109, 174
Govender, Gino 171–172, 175
Government of National Unity *see* GNU
governments 10, 14–15, 70, 73, 98, 109–110
Grameen Bank 134
Grand Rapids, Canada 205–206
green energy *see* renewable energy
greenhouse gas emissions 147, 150, 154, 157
Greenpeace International 171
Group Areas Act 19–20, 187
Growth, Employment and Redistribution
    see GEAR
Gustafsson, Uwe 125–126

Hani, Chris 105–106
Hansen, James 153
Health of Mother Earth Foundation 147
Hogg, David 127
homelands *see* Bantustans
human rights 215–216
hunger 113, 116, 213

Ibrahim, Mo 211
IFP 86–87, 90, 96, 97, 98
IMF 14, 67, 78, 115
immigration to developed world 44
inclusivity 122, 139, 213
India 77–78, 123–132, 197, 214
    see also BRICS
indigenous wisdom 34, 38, 201–207, 213
Indignados movement, Spain 79–80
Industrial Conciliation Act 83–84
industrialisation 64, 203
inequality
    activism and 2–3
    in Africa 110, 167
    financial crisis of 2008 79–81
    impact of 10, 13–17
    reasons for 187–190, 212
    in South Africa 174
    student protests 32–35
information capitalism 78–79
Inkatha Freedom Party *see* IFP

International Energy Agency 157
International Monetary Fund *see* IMF
internet 81, 214
Iraq 69

Kenya 145–146, 159–169, 197
Khoisan 202–204
Kibera, Kenya 165–169, 197
Kilimanjaro *see* Mount Kilimanjaro,
    Tanzania
Korail, Bangladesh 134–139, 197
Kumar, Manoj 124–126
Kumbo, Garam 128–129

labour systems 20–21, 50, 82–83, 162
Lake Turkana, Kenya 145–146
Land Act of 1913 21
land ownership 21, 162–163, 174–181,
    199–200, 209
leaders 7, 75, 80, 92–93, 119, 210, 215–217
Lenin, Vladimir 48
Lephatsi, Jappie 182–186
libraries 166, 194
listening, value of 138, 159, 164–165
loans *see* micro-credit system
local government 180, 193
Lula da Silva, Luiz Inácio 111–114

Maingi, Winifred 163
Mandela, Nelson
  JN and 8–9
  capture 62
  imprisonment 19, 74
  use of force 62, 71
  as leader 69, 103, 112, 130, 168, 172
  on freedom 218
  released from prison 12, 95–96, 185
  transition in South Africa 91, 97, 100
  GNU 104, 108
  death 8
Marcus Garvey Library 166
Marikana shootings 72–73
Marxism 48, 51, 53, 56–57
MDM (Mass Democratic Movement)
  31, 85, 98, 185
Meiners, Christoph 22

Mercredi, Ovide 205–206
micro-credit system 166–167
migrant workers 20–21, 83–84, 176, 183–185
militarism 98
military-industrial complex 73
mines 50, 183–185
mismanagement 180
MK 62–63, 71
mobile technology 81, 156
Mohamed, Pops 202
Mo Ibrahim Foundation 211
Monsanto 127
Mothers' Club 135–138, 167
Mount Kilimanjaro, Tanzania 5–13, 16–17,
  171, 209

Naandi Foundation 123–131
Naidoo, Jay
  family 48, 123
  youth 12, 19–24, 37–38, 187–188
  as student 25–30, 40–42, 47–49
  as volunteer for FOSATU 51–59
  as labourer in textile mill 55–56, 81
  at COSATU 7, 11, 16–17, 31–32, 49–51,
    68, 73–75, 81–82, 85–92, 100
  as member of parliament 104–106
  as communications minister 108,
    155–156
  as minister without portfolio 174
  as board member of Mo Ibrahim
    Foundation 211
  as volunteer in development space
    121–122, 171–172, 175–183, 186
  ascent of Mount Kilimanjaro 5–17,
    171, 209
  visit to Bangladesh 133–143
  visit to Canada 205–206
  visit to Egypt 42–44
  visit to India 123–132
  visit to Kenya 145–146, 159–169
  visit to Namibia 202–204
  visit to Nigeria 147–151
  visit to Soviet Union 68
Naidoo, Kumi 171–172, 175
Naidoo, Logie [brother] 26
Naidoo-Pagé, Kami [son] 6, 16, 112, 202

Naidoo-Pagé, Shanti [daughter] 1
Nairobi, Kenya 159–169
Naledi village 175–183, 186, 190–200, 213
Namibia 202–204
National Party 21, 96
National Peace Accord (NPA) 99–100
National Union of Mineworkers
    see NUM
Native American teaching 199
negotiations 52–53, 91–92
neoliberalism 65–67, 77, 108, 114–116, 118,
    143, 173–175, 212
Nigeria 72, 146–151
Norway, shooting in 72
NP *see* National Party
NPA *see* National Peace Accord
nuclear energy 155
NUM 184
Nyerere, Julius Kambarage 8–9, 197

objectivity 61–62
Occupy Wall Street campaign 24, 80
Odede, Kennedy 165–169
Ogoniland community, Nigeria 148–149
oil reserves 146–149, 151, 167–168
Old Mutual Foundation 192
organic farming 126–128
organising 32, 34, 41–42, 61–62
Outline of History of Mankind, The 22

Pan Africanist Congress (PAC) 39
Paris climate accord 149–150, 152–154
Partido dos Trabalhadores (PT)
    see Workers' Party
passive resistance 31
pass laws 20, 39
patronising attitude 37
Pedagogy of the Oppressed 48
Pieterson, Hector 40
Pitroda, Sam 214–215
police 26, 48, 72–73, 100
    see also security forces
pollution 145, 147, 151, 156
poverty 13–17, 113, 117, 133–134, 195–197,
    210, 216–217
preparedness 16

PT (Partido dos Trabalhadores)
    see Workers' Party
'put up or shut up' point 171

racism 20–22, 31, 33, 41, 72, 92
Rahman, Sheikh Mujibur 134
Rana Plaza disaster 140–142
Rapulome, Justine 194
RDP 106–108, 110, 174–175, 193
Reagan, Ronald 64, 65
recessions 79–81, 111
Reconstruction and Development
    Programme *see* RDP
refugees 157–158
renewable energy 14, 155–158, 194–195,
    213, 215
Reservoir Hills 187–188
Rhodes, Cecil John 20–21, 32–33
#RhodesMustFall campaign 32–33
right-wing politics 70–71, 96–97, 100, 212
Rousseff, Dilma 112, 115–116
Royal Dutch Shell 147, 148–149
Rumuekpe village, Nigeria 147–148
Russia *see* BRICS; Soviet Union
Rustler's Valley Naledi Farmers Co-op 191

SACP 53, 67, 104–106
San 202–204
sanctions against South Africa 64
sanitation *see* toilets
SASO 25–26, 48, 49
Savar, Bangladesh 140–142
schools 124–125, 129–130, 163–164, 168, 178,
    193–195
school shootings in United States 72
seatbelts, campaign for 89
Seattle, Chief 206
security forces 26, 29–30, 48, 62, 72–73,
    96–98, 100
self-sustaining communities 190–192, 213
servant leaders 119
Sharpeville massacre 39–40
Shell 147, 148–149
Shining Hope for Communities
    (SHOFCO) 165–169
shop stewards 52, 93

Snowden, Edward 69
soccer 166
socialism 25, 49–50, 67, 70–71, 82
solar power 155, 157, 194–195, 215
solidarity 63–65, 79, 190
South African Communist Party *see* SACP
South African Students' Organisation
 see SASO
South–South alignment 112, 118
Soviet Union 14, 67–68, 101, 199
 see also BRICS
Soweto uprising 40–42, 44–45, 50
Spain 79–80
state capture 72–73, 109
strikes
 African workers in 1973 38, 47, 50
 miners in 1987 184
student protests 32–34, 40
Sun Tzu 48, 73
Syria 72

Tahrir Square uprising 43–44
Tambo, Oliver 62
technology 2–3, 10, 81–83, 156, 214
Temer, Michel 112
terrorism 62, 69–73, 75
Thatcher, Margaret 64, 65
toilets 160–161
trade agreements 210
trade unions 43, 49–59, 62–63, 74–75,
 77–78, 88–89, 142, 183–185
traditional chiefs 177
transition in South Africa 95–102, 173
tribalism 92, 167
Trotsky, Leon 70–71
Trump, Donald 70, 149–150, 212
Tunisia, uprisings in 23–24
Turner, Rick 49, 51
Tutu, Desmond 69

ubuntu 11, 207, 216
UCT 32–33
UDF 31, 85, 185
Uhuru Peak 6–8, 17
Umkhonto we Sizwe *see* MK
UN *see* United Nations

Unified Workers' Central *see* CUT
uniformity 10
unions 43, 49–59, 62–63, 74–75, 77–78,
 88–89, 142, 183–185
United Democratic Front *see* UDF
United Nations
 Framework Convention on Climate
 Change 152–153
 International Telecommunication
 Union 156
 Millennium Development Goals
 13, 134
 Sustainable Development Goals 152
 UNEP 149
 UNESCO 152
United States of America 62, 68–69, 72,
 78, 80–81
United Workers' Union of South Africa
 see UWUSA
unity 74–75, 92
University of Cape Town *see* UCT
University of Durban-Westville 40–41
USA *see* United States of America
UWUSA 87

vandalism *see* burning down of facilities
vigilance 15, 109–110
violence 31, 90–91, 96–100
Vuwani, Limpopo 90

Washington Consensus 78
water, access to 129, 179–180, 193
Weru, Jane 162–163
Western cultural norms 10–11, 23, 34, 216
What Is to be Done? 48
wind energy 157
wisdom from ancient cultures 34, 38,
 201–207, 213
women's empowerment 124, 131,
 134–140, 167
Workers' Party (Brazil) 111–112, 115–118
'Working for Water' project 193
World Bank 14, 43, 67, 78, 115, 155
World Trade Organization 78
World Wide Fund for Nature 150
Wretched of the Earth, The 48

youth
  activism 2–4, 213–214
  childhood deaths 209–210
  education 124, 139–140
  employment 82–83, 139–140
  extremist groups and 71–72

Grand Rapids, Manitoba 205
  population 168, 209
Yunus, Muhammad 134, 137

Zero Hunger campaign 113, 116
Zorg van de Zaak 192